DARK FILES

Book 1
A Pictorial History of Lost,
Forgotten, and Obscure
UFO Encounters

Michael Schratt

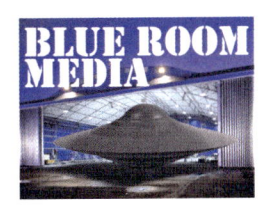

BLUE ROOM MEDIA

First Edtion Copyright © 2022 Michael Schratt

All rights reserved. This book or any portion thereof may not be reproduced or used in any manner whatsoever without the express written permission of the author except for the use of brief quotations in a book review.

First Edition, First Printing, 2022

ISBN 978-0-578-36926-6

Cover and inside text layouts by Gordon Bond Designs
Fonts: headlines, Armalite Rifle; text, Linux Libertine

This book is dedicated to:

Jim Goodall

*author, researcher, historian, maverick, chaser of "spooky aircraft"
and things that go "bump in the night."*

Thanks for your friendship, support, inspiration and believing in me.

FOREWORD

Michael Schratt has been an important figure in UFOlogy for years—a devoted and indefatigable researcher.

In Dark Files, he has done for UFOlogy what Ansel Adams did for Yosemite—he has brought it to life. With the summaries, the engineering-quality drawings that he created, and the color illustrations he commissioned, these cases simply jump off the pages.

In so doing, he has made these cases effectively available to more than the handful of researchers who have read the written descriptions themselves.

So, enjoy the wonderful work that Michael has poured into Dark Files.

We're lucky to have Michael in the field, and I'm honored to call him my friend.

Paul Hynek
Los Angeles
July, 2020

ACKNOWLEDGEMENTS

I would like to acknowledge the following individuals: Mark Rodeghier, CUFOS director, who was a great help by allowing me to access the entire CUFOS Library/archives for well over two years. Tom Bogan, your artwork has made the cases in this book truly "come alive." I could not have done it without you. Richard and Tracey Dolan, your tireless contribution to this field can truly never be measured. Thanks for inspiring me, supporting me, and giving me a platform to contribute to this field. Richard, you are a gentleman and a scholar. Mark Mikowski, thanks for your friendship, help and support. Norio Hayakawa, a true pioneer, thanks for your inspiration, help and support. Dan Benkert, always nice to speak to someone that has the same level of interest. Linda Zimmerman (author and researcher), the depth of your knowledge is incredible. Thanks for helping me. Jim Nichols (artist, researcher and lecturer), thanks for being a great friend. Annabelle and Dale, I feel like I have known the both of you my whole life. Thanks for your encouragement. David Marler, thanks to absolutely one of the best researchers in the field. Thanks for letting me review your historical files. Stacey Wright, thanks for believing in me, and giving me a platform to speak. Jim Mann, thanks for your kindness and help. Harry Drew, (author and historian), the absolute definition of a researcher that pays attention to the details. Thanks for your help. Richard C. Hoagland, your presentations have inspired multiple generations. Scott and Suzanne Ramsey, leading researchers in this field. Thanks for your help. John Andrews, A true trail blazer, class act, and one of the nicest people I ever had the honor to meet. Special thanks to Robert A. (who ultimately made this research effort possible).

Note: All illustrations/artwork by Tom Bogan, Michael Schratt, John MacNeill and Rudy Gardea.

INTRODUCTION

Well folks, I finally did it. After spending 26 years compiling UFO case files, eyewitness reports, video tape interviews, drawings, sketches and illustrations, I decided it was time to "land the plane," and put these reports "down on paper." Hopefully, this will be the first in a series of fully illustrated volumes which endeavors to preserve an important part of our national history. All of the cases contained in this publication include paperwork/documentation and their associated sources so you can verify them on your own. I made the decision to start this series in an effort to make these cases "come alive," rather than allow them to fade away to history in a dark and dusty archive/warehouse.

These cases span from the "Mystery Airship wave of 1897" to a bizarre encounter with a triangular "water pumper" UFO seen at the little Pudding River in Oregon in 2012. Although separated by time and space, a strange sense of "pattern recognition" has emerged after examining these cases. In other words, distinctive features on UFOs reported by eyewitnesses from one part of the country appears to have been "mirrored" on separate craft thousands of miles away. These features include "tubes, pipes and cylinders," rivets, "prongs/protrusions," high pitched "drilling" sounds, low frequency "humming" noises and your typical CEII effects.

In addition, "beings" associated with these craft also appear to have their own similarities which include the following: seamless one-piece tight-fitting flight suits, "cone shaped" hands, helmets that extend down to the shoulders, "Michelin Man" space suits, laughter, and gestures of "waving back." Do these beings originate from a previously unknown high-tech advanced society already on this planet, or does the real truth lie somewhere much closer than we realize?

I invite you to join me on this fascinating journey, and perhaps we can shatter the "Cosmic Watergate" as a united coalition of inquisitive researchers.

Michael Schratt
undisclosed location
July 2020

TABLE OF CONTENTS

OTTO BINDER AND CARL PFEUFER 1
EARLY UFO OCCUPANT SIGHTING Bay of Fundy, October 12, 1796 2
"CUBE SHAPED" UFO SIGHTED November 13, 1833, Niagara Falls 3
THE "ARMOR PLATED FLYING MACHINE" July 1868, Capiago, Chile 4
STRANGER ON THE OCEAN 1882, near Ascension Isle 5
THE 1897 MYSTERY AIRSHIP WAVE 6
"BOAT SHAPED" UFO SIGHTED July 30, 1909 9
UFO ENCOUNTER OVER SNAKE RIVER CANYON August 13, 1947, Twin Falls, ID 10
MISSILE TEST INTERRUPTED June 14, 1949, White Sands Missile Range 11
"EXPERIMENTAL AIRCRAFT" SIGHTED BY PILOTS March 21, 1950, Stuttgart, AR 12
AIRLINER ENCOUNTERS CIGAR SHAPED UFO January 20, 1951, Sioux City, IA 14
FAILED INTERCEPT 1951, West German airbase 15
THE "RINGED CIGAR UFO" June 1953, Saugerties, NY 16
THE FLYING "VANITY LIGHT" November 20, 1956, Danielson, CT 19
CAUGHT ON FILM 1957, Edwards Air Force Base, CA 22
USS *FRANKLIN D. ROOSEVELT* ENCOUNTERS CIGAR-SHAPED UFO
   Late 1958, Off Guantanamo Bay, Cuba 24
FISHING BOAT CREW SPOTS DIVING UFOS April 19, 1959, near Japan 28
"THEY WAVED BACK," THE FATHER GILL CASE June 26, 1959, Papua, New Guinea 29
COUNTER ROTATING FLAMING JET UFO July 13, 1959, Blenheim, New Zealand 31
AUTOMOBILE LEVITATION 1961, Stigler, OK 35
UNDERWATER MOTORBOAT SURPRISE June 3, 1961, Savona, Italy 36
NAVAL TEST INTERRUPTED 1963, Puerto Rico 37
A SURPRISE VISIT October 2, 1962, off the coast of Sardinia, west of Italy 38
THE SOCORRO LANDING April 24, 1964, Socorro, NM 39
"FLAMING TOP" UFO June 29, 1964, Lavonia, GA 42
"BEEHIVE" UFO ENCOUNTER December 21, 1964, Fishersville, VA 43
A MOST CURIOUS MORNING COMMUTE March 23, 1966, Temple, OK 44
RECESS INTERRUPTED April 6, 1966 Melbourne, Australia 46
"STOP THE PRESS" October 26, 1966 49
"TIC-TAC" UAP ENCOUNTER March 1967, Wycombe, PA 50
WEEKEND PROSPECTING INTERRUPTED
   May 19, 1967, Falcon Lake, Manitoba, Canada 52

A MOST INTERESTING FISHING TRIP *May 1967, Hartwell Lake, Anderson, SC* 56
"FAT FRISBEE" OVER DETROIT *July 1967* 57
THE EMERGING TURQUOISE BALL *August 4, 1967, Gulf north of Arrecife, Venezuela* ... 58
THE CHAOTIC CASE OF THE "VENT UFO" *August 1967* 59
GLOBE SHAPED UFO WITH TRANSPARENT DOME *January 24, 1968, Indiana, PA* 60
THE "FLAMING SKULL" UFO *May 6, 1968, Elyria, OH* 61
"MICHELIN MAN" ENCOUNTER *July 31, 1968, Reunion Island* 62
HELICOPTER SURPRISE *September 9, 1968, Dong Ha, Viet Nam* 63
CHILLY ENCOUNTER ON THE SLOPES *January 7, 1970, Heinola, Finland* 64
THE FLYING IRON *October 9, 1972, Long Island, NY* 66
"THE FLAMING ELLIPSE" *December 26, 1972, Maracaibo, Venezuela* 68
U.S. ARMY RESERVE HELICOPTER UFO ENCOUNTER
  October 18, 1973, Mansfield, OH 71
"SUNDAY NIGHT AT THE OSCARS" MICHELIN MAN CASE #2
  March 14, 1976, Liria, Spain 73
"GLASS BUBBLE" UFO WITH OCCUPANTS *June 22, 1976, Canary Islands* 75
"FAT FRISBEE" SIGHTING #2 *December 1976, Dana Point, CA* 78
THE "ORANGE JUICER" WITH TENTACLES *September 10, 1976, Colusa, CA* 81
A BELL IN THE BACKYARD *November 6, 1976, Virginia Beach, VA* 85
SIGHTING OF INFLATABLE BEING IN CAPSULE *February 10, 1977, Tucson, AZ* 86
UFO ENCOUNTER WITH CEII EFFECTS *January 1978, Fort Smith, AR* 89
FARM LANDING SURPRISE *May 1978, Weeley, England* 90
SAUCER WITH PIPE ENCOUNTER *September 11, 1980, Anderson, SC* 91
STRANGE ENCOUNTER WITH OCCUPANTS OVER ALABAMA
  February 3, 1983, Mobile, AL 93
"MOTHERSHIP" SIGHTED BY AIRLINE CAPTAIN *November 17, 1986, Eastern, AK* 95
CONNING TOWER UFO *May 14, 1988, Gresham, OR* 99
SURPRISE LAUNCH AT SEA *February 7, 1989, Catalina Island* 104
THE FYING USO ARMADA *June 14, 1992, Catalina Island* 105
THE FYING "MIDAS MUFFLER SHOP" *November 1994, Buxton, England* 106
MOTORCYCLE STALLED BY "FLYING PYRAMID" *1994, Uttoxeter, England* 107
EGG SHAPE "PINCER" USO ENCOUNTER. *August 1997, Monterey Bay, CA* 108
SAUCER WITH "OCTOPUS TENTACLES" SEEN AT O'HARE
  April/May 2001, O'Hare Airport, Chicago, IL 111
THE TRIANGULAR "WATER PUMPER" UFO *2012, Little Pudding River, Oregon* 113
ABOUT THE AUTHOR 115

OTTO BINDER AND CARL PFEUFER

Otto Binder (left, 1911-1974) was a prolific writer from Chicago, who moved to New York in 1936. He is best known as the co-creator of Supergirl and for his many scripts for *Captain Marvel Adventures and* other stories involving the entire superhero Marvel Family. He was prolific in the comic book field and is credited with writing over 4,400 stories across a variety of publishers under his own name, as well as more than 160 stories under the pen-name Eando Binder. From 1965 to 1969, he published a weekly newspaper column titled "Our Space Age," which was published in 25 states, and 11 foreign newspapers. This unique weekly column featured non-fiction UFO reports from all around the world, each including a brief historical background and a very well-done drawing by artist **Carl Pfeufer** (lower right, 1910-1980).

Pfeufer was an American comic-book artist, magazine illustrator, painter, and sculptor. He was an early contributor to American comic books; one of the primary early artists of the Marvel Comics superhero the Sub-Mariner; and the longtime artist of Western hero Tom Mix's comic books.

The "Our Space Age" reports included many classic UFO cases, as well as new accounts sent to him by readers.

This author has included 10 of Otto Binder's original cases files which have been illustrated in full color for the very first time by Tom Bogan.

Sources: Gray Barker UFO Collection (Clarksburg, WV); wikipedia.com.

EARLY UFO OCCUPANT SIGHTING
Bay of Fundy, October 12, 1796

OCT. 12, 1796...
ON COLUMBUS DAY OVER 170 YEARS AGO, CANADIAN OBSERVERS REPORTED AN ASTONISHING FLEET OF AIRSHIPS (UFO'S), WITH PORTHOLES AND VISIBLE OCCUPANTS, SAILING OVER THE BAY OF FUNDY.

"CUBE SHAPED" UFO SIGHTED

November 13, 1833, Niagara Falls

NOV. 13, 1833...
A CROWD ON BOTH THE AMERICAN AND CANADIAN SIDES SAW A PECULIAR SQUARE-SHAPED UFO HOVER OVER NIAGARA FALLS FOR AN HOUR, AFTER WHICH IT SPED AWAY TOWARD THE OCEAN.

READERS! SEE YOUR SIGHTING ILLUSTRATED HERE! SEND YOUR UFO REPORT IN DETAIL PLUS SKETCH TO... OTTO BINDER, "OUR SPACE AGE,"

DO NOT THROW STONES OVER THE CLIFF.

THE "ARMOR PLATED FLYING MACHINE"
July 1868, Capiago, Chile

JULY, 1868... VILLAGERS IN CAPIAGO, CHILE, WERE FRIGHTENED BY A GIANT "ARMOR-PLATED" MACHINE COVERED WITH "STEEL SCALES", WHOSE TWIN SEARCHLIGHT "EYES" STABBED DOWN BRILLIANTLY!

Bogan

STRANGER ON THE OCEAN
1882, near Ascension Isle

1882, NEAR ASCENSION ISLE...
A BRITISH STEAMER CAME UPON A GIGANTIC UFO FLOATING IN THE OCEAN, AT LEAST 800 FEET LONG OR NEARLY AS BIG AS THE QUEEN ELIZABETH, WHICH SLOWLY SANK BENEATH THE WAVES AND VANISHED FROM SIGHT.

THE 1897 MYSTERY AIRSHIP WAVE

On the evening of November 18, 1896 hundreds of residents in Sacramento, California, sighted a strange cylindrical-shaped craft gliding through the sky. The object cast down brilliant beams of light on the city below, and then proceeded towards San Francisco. The following evening, the bay communities of Oakland and San Francisco were plunged into chaos. Horses bolted, buggies overturned, and people were panicking in the streets. Another mysterious flying craft made a low pass over the streets before it headed out towards the coast and disappeared.

Although these events technically began in the year 1896, this specific flap of sightings has always generally been referred to as the "Mystery Airship wave of 1897." In a desperate effort to make sense of the sightings, newspapers from California to West Virginia published literally hundreds of articles on the subject which can still be accessed today.

Descriptions of the craft varied between sightings, but most reports included details of a craft that was approximately 150 feet in length. It had "bird-like" wings and a tail, with "rotor-like" arms. Powerful beams of light were seen shining down from the craft. In many cases, an "airbag" could be seen which supported a "gondola" with windows from above. In some cases, eyewitnesses reported seeing what looked like "well dressed inventor" type men on the upper deck, with "big black dogs." In addition, there were multiple reports of "laughter" coming from the craft, and in some cases, "anchors" were lowered to the ground. In other instances, these mysterious airships landed with "normal looking humans" that stepped out. Witnesses who spoke to the "pilots" claimed that they had somehow cracked the secret of "*gravity control*" since they didn't use hot air or helium for "lift." Some of the mysterious airships were reported to have been travelling at a speed of over 50 mph *against the wind,* (all before the Wright Brothers first flight on December 17, 1903).

By December of 1896, sighting reports completely disappeared, but by March of 1897, the aerial performers returned. On April 11, 1897 *The New York Herald* reported that on the nights of April 9 and 10, Chicago was flooded with accounts of strange lights that were seen from 8:00 p.m., until 2:00 a.m. Eyewitnesses stated that they could see two "cigar-shaped" objects with great wings. At Sisterville, West Virginia, a luminous red object flew in from the northwest at about 9:00 p.m. on the night of April 19. It beamed brilliant spotlights on the town below, throwing the village into havoc. The sawmill whistle was blowing frantically as hundreds of people rushed into the streets to get a glimpse of the craft. It was described as looking like an "immense cigar," with two protruding fins on either side. Observers estimated to have been 180 feet in length. All of the witnesses could clearly see flashing red, white and green lights along the sides and stern.

On April 22, 1897 *The Arkansas Gazette* published an amazing account by Captain Jim Hooten who was a well-known railroad conductor. Captain Hooten was hunting near Homan, Arkansas, when it started getting dark. As he began walking back to the railway station, he recognized a familiar sound, like the noise of a locomotive air-pump or Westinghouse air-brake. Suddenly, he came across five men repairing an odd-looking machine. One of them was wearing "smoked glasses." Captain Hooten stated that the front of the strange craft ended in an abrupt knife-like edge. The sides bulged outward, and then tapered back. There were three large wheels on each side. Shortly thereafter, the craft rose with a "*hissing"* (emphasis added throughout to indicate features common to many witness accounts) sound and disappeared from sight.

Although the "Mystery Airship wave of 1897" was never conclusively solved, author and researcher Walter Bosley makes a great case for a very terrestrial explanation. In his book *Origin, The Nineteenth Century Emergence of the 20th Century Breakaway Civilizations*, Bosley lays out a well-researched historical account of the secret activities pertaining to the "Sonora Aero Club." This group of eccentric and intellectual inventors met in California in 1850, and began experimenting with strange and fantastic flying machines. They were said to have been financed by a mysterious group known only as "NYMZA." [Sources: *Far Out,* Spring 1993, *Flying Saucer Review,* Vol. 34, No. 3 1989, *Flying Saucer Review,* Vol. 13, No. 4 1967, *Flying Saucer Review* Vol. 11, No. 5 1966, *Flying Saucer Review,* Vol. 12, No. 4 1966, *Saint Louis Post Dispatch* April 14, 1897, *Saucer News* Vol. 17 No. 1 1970.]

"BOAT SHAPED" UFO SIGHTED

July 30, 1909

JULY 30, 1909.
WAIKAKA VALLEY, N.Z. ... MEN ABOARD A DREDGE REPORTED A BOAT-SHAPED UFO THAT CIRCLED ALL AROUND, WITH TWO HUMANLIKE FIGURES VISIBLE INSIDE.

UFO ENCOUNTER OVER SNAKE RIVER CANYON

August 13, 1947, Twin Falls, ID

On August 13, 1947, a farmer, A.C. Urie, and his two sons (ages eight and ten), were in the Snake River Canyon (Twin Falls, Idaho, region), around 1:00 p.m., when they observed an unusual object flying between the canyon walls. Mr. Urie was on land, while his two sons were in a boat approximately 300 feet away. The strange UFO was not saucer shaped, but resembled an elliptical or oblong, broad-brimmed hat, with a low crown. It measured approximately 25 feet across, and ten feet thick at the center. The main body of the craft resembled an inverted pie-plate. Its outer edge appeared to be about one foot thick, and strange "flames" emanated out of single "engines pods" which were located on each side of the craft. The UFO was flying approximately 300 feet below the rim of the canyon. According to the three eyewitnesses involved, the flame left no smoke or contrail behind. The UFO was estimated to be travelling at a speed of 1,000 mph, and moving from the east to the west. The primary eyewitness stated that the vehicle only emitted a faint "swishing" sound, and in his assessment used some type of atomic energy as its power source. [Sources: NICAP, *Twin Falls Times News* August 15, 1947, United States Air Force Project Blue Book Special Report #14]

MISSILE TEST INTERRUPTED
June 14, 1949, White Sands Missile Range

On June 14, 1949, a significant UFO encounter took place at White Sands missile range in New Mexico. A crew of Navy engineers and technicians under the direction of Commander Robert B. McLaughlin were conducting an upper atmospheric test, when the missile they had launched was joined (one on each side) by two unknown silver-colored metallic spheres which were approximately 20 inches in diameter. During its ascent, the missile had attained a speed of 2,000 feet per second (equivalent to 1,363 mph). Soon thereafter, the circular shaped object on the left broke formation, descended below the missile, and passed directly through the missile's exhaust. Then, the strange object joined the other unknown spherical shaped UFO, and together they accelerated upwards *leaving the missile behind.*

Shortly after the encounter, Commander McLaughlin received independent confirmation from five separate observation posts that also witnessed the unusual event. To date, no *known* government has been identified which had the technology (in 1949) to build vehicles that look or fly like the ones mentioned in this case. Author's special note: Could there be a Nazi connection to this mysterious case as reported in the New York Times on December 14, 1944? *Floating Mystery Ball Is New Nazi Air Weapon.* [Sources: NICAP, Uninvited Guests by Richard Hall]

"EXPERIMENTAL AIRCRAFT" SIGHTED BY PILOTS
March 21, 1950, Stuttgart, AR

March 21, 1950 Captain Jack Adams and 1st Officer G.W. Anderson were flying 15 miles north of Stuttgart, Arkansas, at an altitude of 2,000 feet. They were on a commercial flight from Memphis to Houston. The visibility and ceiling were unlimited, and the sky was clear. It was 9:29 p.m., when both pilots observed 95-foot diameter disc shaped craft with red and green running lights. The object was flying at a speed of approximately 600 mph, and passed in front of their DC-3 at an altitude of 3,000 feet. The object remained in full view for about 30 seconds, and both pilots got a good look at it. Ten illuminated port holes could be seen on its bottom surface. The strange craft also had a very rapidly blinking blue/white light on top. No exhaust or vapor tail could be seen coming from the object.

Captain Adams commented: "I believe it was some kind of experimental type aircraft that has been kept a secret by the Air Force. It was definitely some kind of aircraft in controlled flight moving at tremendous speed." Captain Adams went on to state that "we firmly believe that the flying saucer we saw over Arkansas Monday night was a secret experimental type aircraft, not a visitor from outer space." Both pilots had over 6,000 hours of flying time each on the day of the sighting. Author's special note: It's interesting to note that both pilots were contacted by Air Force Intelligence for questioning after landing in Houston. [Sources: *Northwest Arkansas Times* March 22, 1950, *Asheville Citizen Times* March 22, 1950]

FLIGHT CREW FLYING SAUCER SIGHTING
(MARCH 21, 1950 STUTTGART ARKANSAS)

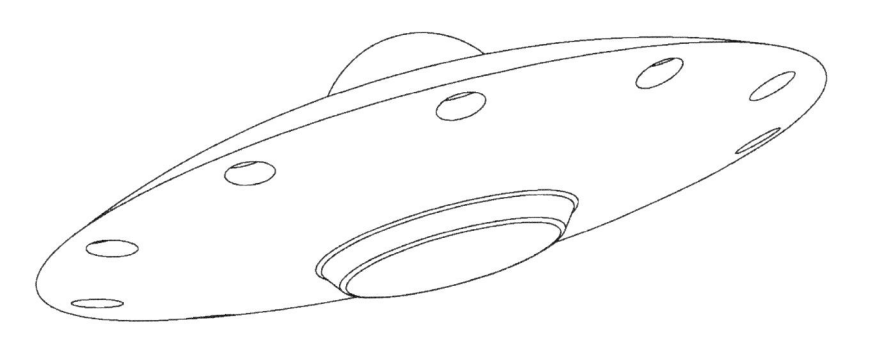

SIGHTING TOOK PLACE AT 9:29 PM, 15 MILES NORTH OF STUTTGART ARKANSAS
OBJECT HAD CONVENTIONAL LOOKING GREEN AND RED RUNNING LIGHTS
SIGHTING TOOK PLACE AT AT AN ALTITUDE OF 2,000 FEET
THE CRAFT WAS FLYING AT TREMENDOUS SPEED (600 MPH) AND LEFT NO VAPOR TRAIL
BOTH PILOTS COULD SEE 10 ILLUMINATED CIRCULAR PORTS ON THE BOTTOM OF THE CRAFT

"WE FIRMLY BELIEVE THAT THE FLYING SAUCER WE SAW OVER ARKANSAS MONDAY NIGHT WAS A SECRET EXPERIMENTAL TYPE AIRCRAFT, NOT A VISITOR FROM OUTER SPACE."
(CAPTAIN JACK ADAMS AND FIRST OFFICER G.W. ANDERSON)

"I BELIEVE IT WAS SOME KIND OF EXPERIMENTAL TYPE AIRCRAFT THAT HAS BEEN KEPT A SECRET BY THE AIR FORCE, IT WAS DEFINITELY SOME KIND OF AIRCRAFT IN CONTROLLED FLIGHT MOVING AT TREMENDOUS SPEED" - CAPTAIN JACK ADAMS

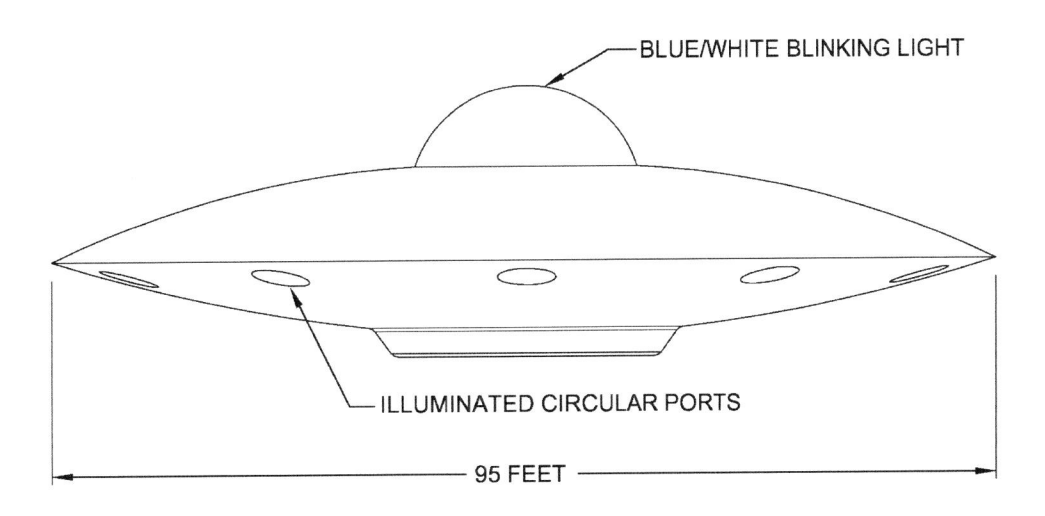

BLUE/WHITE BLINKING LIGHT
ILLUMINATED CIRCULAR PORTS
95 FEET

DRAWN BY: MICHAEL SCHRATT 4/21/21

AIRLINER ENCOUNTERS CIGAR SHAPED UFO
January 20, 1951, Sioux City, IA

JAN. 20, 1951 NEAR SIOUX CITY, IOWA... A HUGE, CIGAR-SHAPED UFO ZOOMED STRAIGHT AT AN AIRLINER, THEN INCREDIBLY MADE A SHARP HAIRPIN TURN AND SPED BACK THE WAY IT HAD COME, ALL IN SHORT SECONDS.

FAILED INTERCEPT
1951, West German airbase

It was 1951 when pilot (later astronaut) Gordon Cooper was alerted to a fleet of flying saucers which had flown over the West German air base where he was stationed. For two consecutive weeks, the base meteorologist had tracked the unknown craft flying at high altitude. By the second week, Gordon Cooper decided it was time to investigate further. Climbing into the cockpit of his F-86 Sabre, with his wingman by his side, both took off and quickly attained a high angle of attack for an attempted intercept of the strange UFOs.

However, it quickly became apparent to both pilots that chasing after the unknown objects would prove to be very difficult. The UFOs were described as being saucer in shape with a dome on top. They had a silver-colored metallic exterior appearance. In addition, the unknown objects could stop in mid-flight, make 90 degree turns and even fly backwards. Later in 1978, Gordon Cooper wrote a letter to the United Nations detailing his encounter. [Sources: "Leap of Faith" by Gordon Cooper, *Corvallis Gazette Times,* October 11, 2000.]

THE "RINGED CIGAR UFO"
June 1953, Saugerties, NY

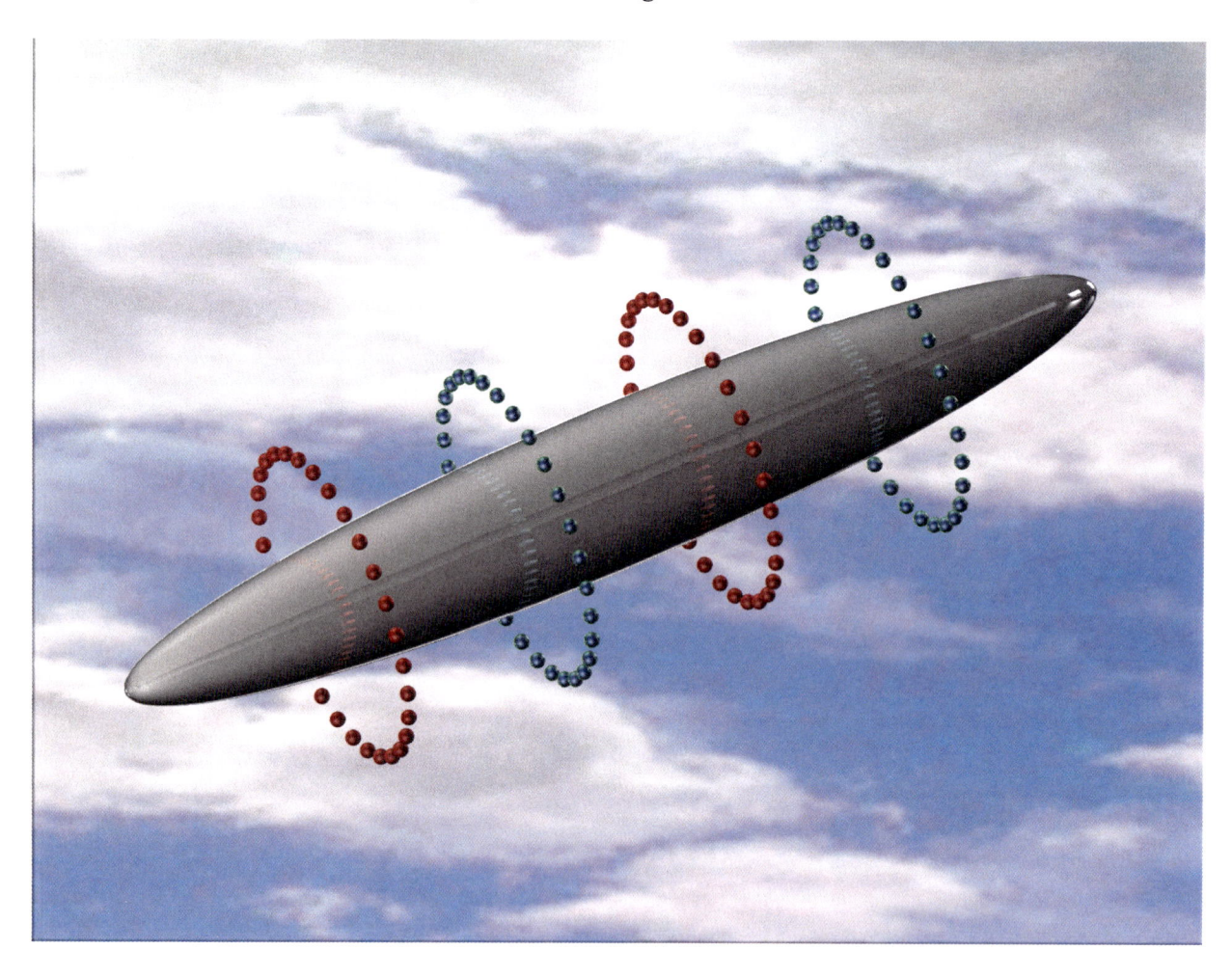

During June of 1953, a group of approximately 12 eyewitnesses observed something truly incredible in the sky above Saugerties, New York. A very large "cigar shaped" UFO measuring 300-350 feet in length was seen during daylight hours. The strange craft had multiple concentric rings made of orbs, that were oriented along its length. The rings had an alternating red and turquoise appearance. It had a brushed aluminum exterior surface. After approximately 10 minutes, two USAF F-86 Sabre jets attempted and intercept, but were abruptly left behind as the craft departed like a spark off a grinding wheel. [Source: "In the Night Sky" by Linda Zimmermann]

CIGAR SHAPED CRAFT WITH RINGS
SIGHTED IN JUNE OF 1953 SAUGERTIES NY.
(PRIMARY EYEWITNESS: HANK VANDERBECK)

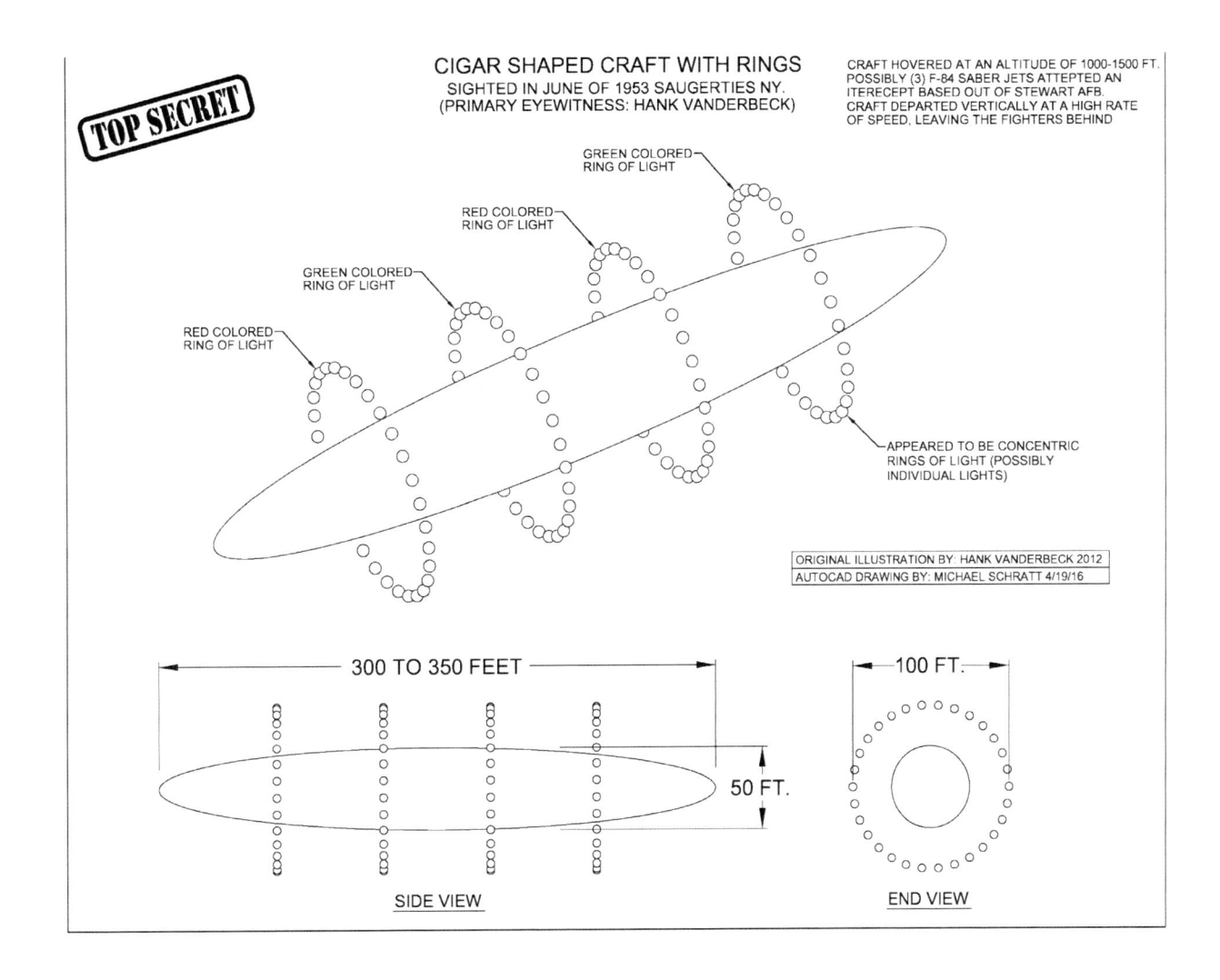

CRAFT HOVERED AT AN ALTITUDE OF 1000-1500 FT. POSSIBLY (3) F-84 SABER JETS ATTEPTED AN ITERECEPT BASED OUT OF STEWART AFB. CRAFT DEPARTED VERTICALLY AT A HIGH RATE OF SPEED, LEAVING THE FIGHTERS BEHIND

TOP SECRET

- GREEN COLORED RING OF LIGHT
- RED COLORED RING OF LIGHT
- GREEN COLORED RING OF LIGHT
- RED COLORED RING OF LIGHT
- APPEARED TO BE CONCENTRIC RINGS OF LIGHT (POSSIBLY INDIVIDUAL LIGHTS)

ORIGINAL ILLUSTRATION BY: HANK VANDERBECK 2012
AUTOCAD DRAWING BY: MICHAEL SCHRATT 4/19/16

300 TO 350 FEET

50 FT.

100 FT.

SIDE VIEW

END VIEW

Drawing by Rudy Gardea

THE FLYING "VANITY LIGHT"
November 20, 1956, Danielson, CT

On November 20, 1956 Elsie Krajewski of Danielson, Connecticut, went outside to hang up clothes to dry. It was very late in the evening, and her three young children were asleep inside. Suddenly, she saw a series of lights moving near the horizon to the north. Soon after, the lights started approaching closer and she initially thought they might be from a nearby aircraft. Then, Elise noticed a structured craft that was in the form of a half sphere with yellow light emanating from inside. It looked like it was made from one solid piece of material, and it had no seams or openings. There were a series of multi-colored lights near the bottom which were rotating at a slow rate of speed. Then the object moved downward as if it was going to land, but stopped just short of the ground. Next the craft rose up and barely cleared the roof of her house. Ms. Krajewski described it as being approximately 25 feet across and 10 feet high. There were absolutely no doors, windows or seams of any kind. She also noticed that the craft emitted no noise whatsoever.

At this point she observed the "sockets" which were gold in color. These looked like three stacked doughnuts separated by two black bands. There was a colored bulb in the bottom of each socket. On bottom side of each "doughnut," there was a design which looked like Arabic writing which consisted of curved lines, dots and dashes. Ms. Krajewski commented that the designs resembled the exterior borders of Oriental or Persian rugs. They also resembled designs seen on Mayan, Aztec, or Inca pottery and blankets. The inscriptions on all the gold rings were identical. There were a total of 24 sockets, each containing a different colored bulb (red, green, blue, orange, yellow, and white). The pattern of the sockets repeated, and all were connected to a translucent sub-floor which was indented two feet up inside the rim of the craft. After a few minutes, the craft dropped to an altitude of about eight feet, and continued down a nearby road until it was no longer in view. [Source: Wendelle Stevens UFO collection]

20

Detail view of "sockets" with "donuts" and black colored bands as described by Elsie Krajewski

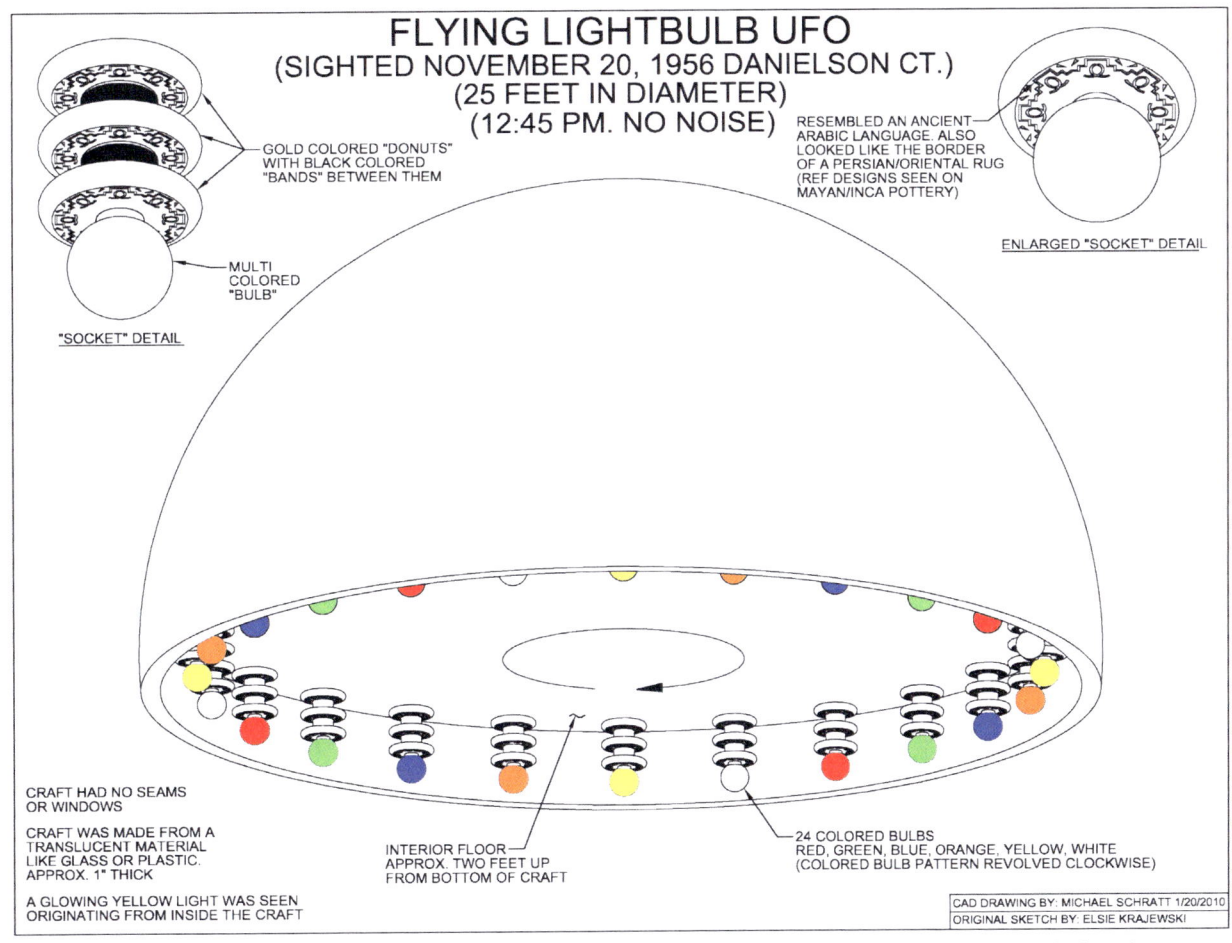

Flying "vanity light" drawing by Michael Schratt based from Elsie Krajewski original sketch

CAUGHT ON FILM
1957, Edwards Air Force Base, CA

    It was May 3, 1957 when two official Air Force photographers, James Bittick and Jack Gettys, were filming the installation of an Askania Cinetheodolite (precision landing equipment) on Rogers Dry Lake in the Mojave Desert of Kern County, California. They had both still and motion picture cameras. Suddenly, a metallic disc shaped craft appeared that measured approximately 25 feet in diameter. The craft had a small dome on top, with extendable tripod landing gear legs. After hovering for a few moments above the surface of the lakebed, the strange object extended its landing gear and landed. The two cameramen were approximately 50 yards away. The UFO remained stationary for approximately 60 seconds, then lifted off and retracted its gear. At that point, the object departed the area. Both cameramen witnessed the entire event, and captured the flying saucer on motion picture and still print film. The film was brought back to the main part of the base, and Gordon Cooper was alerted to the situation.

The Pentagon was informed, and issued the directive to develop the film, but "do not make prints." Cooper followed orders, but did look at the negative print film, and motion picture footage. The quality of the film was good, but he did not run it through a projector. He was then instructed to seal all of the film in a specially locked courier pouch and send it directly to the Pentagon. Author's special note: Where did the film eventually end up? Who has jurisdiction over this historic piece of footage? Are there other official USAF/US NAVY photos and film reels hidden away in a secret underground bunker or warehouse? [Sources: "Leap of Faith" by Gordon Cooper, *Corvallis Gazette Times*, October 11, 2004]

USS *FRANKLIN D. ROOSEVELT* ENCOUNTERS CIGAR-SHAPED UFO

Late 1958, Off Guantanamo Bay, Cuba

Late in 1958, a startling event involving a cigar-shaped UFO, and the Midway class aircraft carrier USS *Franklin D. Roosevelt* (CVA-42), took place off Guantanamo Bay, Cuba. This report originated from Chester Grusinski, who was a fireman's apprentice onboard the carrier when the event occurred. The *Roosevelt* was on a shakedown cruise, when around 9:00 p.m., a significant commotion began to spread below decks. Naval personnel began rushing up the ladder to the flight deck. Once "top side," at least 25 eyewitnesses reported seeing a small light which appeared to be following the ship, and approached the carrier at an incredible speed. The strange craft made no sound whatsoever, and maneuvered unlike any known aircraft. As the object descended to within approximately 100 feet above the flight deck, its cigar-shaped appearance was now clearly visible (see original MUFON report sketch). The craft appeared to be about 100 feet in length, and had a row of widows which were lit from inside running along its length. A number of "figures" could be seen, who were observing the officers on the flight deck below. Many of the witnesses reported seeing what looked like heat distortion waves coming from the craft, and they recalled feeling a warm sensation on their faces.

As the unknown craft departed, it turned a red-orange color, and rose vertically at a high rate of speed. In an official effort by the United States Navy to bury this event, most of the eyewitnesses were quickly transferred off the *Roosevelt*, and the ship's log-books were altered. An interesting historical note to this case included in the original report, indicated that this was not the first encounter that the USS *Franklin D. Roosevelt* had with UFOs. Indeed, during "Operation Mainbrace" in 1952, photos of a UFO were taken from the deck of the ship. Two additional sightings involving the ship occurred in 1956, while it was at anchor in the port of Rio de Janeiro. A final sighting also took place in 1973. One possible explanation as to why the *Roosevelt* had so many sightings may be due to the fact that it was the first aircraft carrier allowed to utilize nuclear weapons on a full-time basis. The fact that there were multiple eyewitnesses, and that the object was tracked by the ship's radar, make this one of the strongest cases in Ufology. [Source: CUFOS archives, MUFON archives, *Motor City News*, August 17, 1998, *Broad Top Bulletin*, December 1, 1999, *Broad Top Bulletin*, December 26, 2000]

Chaos erupts on the flight deck of the USS Franklin D. Roosevelt *during a shocking UFO encounter in late 1958.*

Enlarged view of "being" waving back to the crew on flight deck below

Author's special note: Since this encounter included both physical effects and a visible sighting of beings of unknown origin, it falls under the category of both a close encounter of the second and third kind. After the sighting, special investigators came aboard (including the CIA). Obviously, they were interested in interviewing the captain and obtaining any documented evidence on the encounter including the ship's logbooks. In addition, since the craft was being tracked by the ship's radar, those records would have been of very special interest to the intelligence community. The excuse they made for the inquiry was "gambling below decks." Where are these files now? What happened to the logbooks and radar tapes? Are they under the jurisdiction of the United States Navy in an underground vault below the Pentagon? What high resolution photography and motion picture film footage of UFOs has the Navy acquired after 75 over the past? Students of ufology have long known that it has always been the U.S. Navy that was "pulling the strings" behind the scenes, and not necessarily the Air Force.

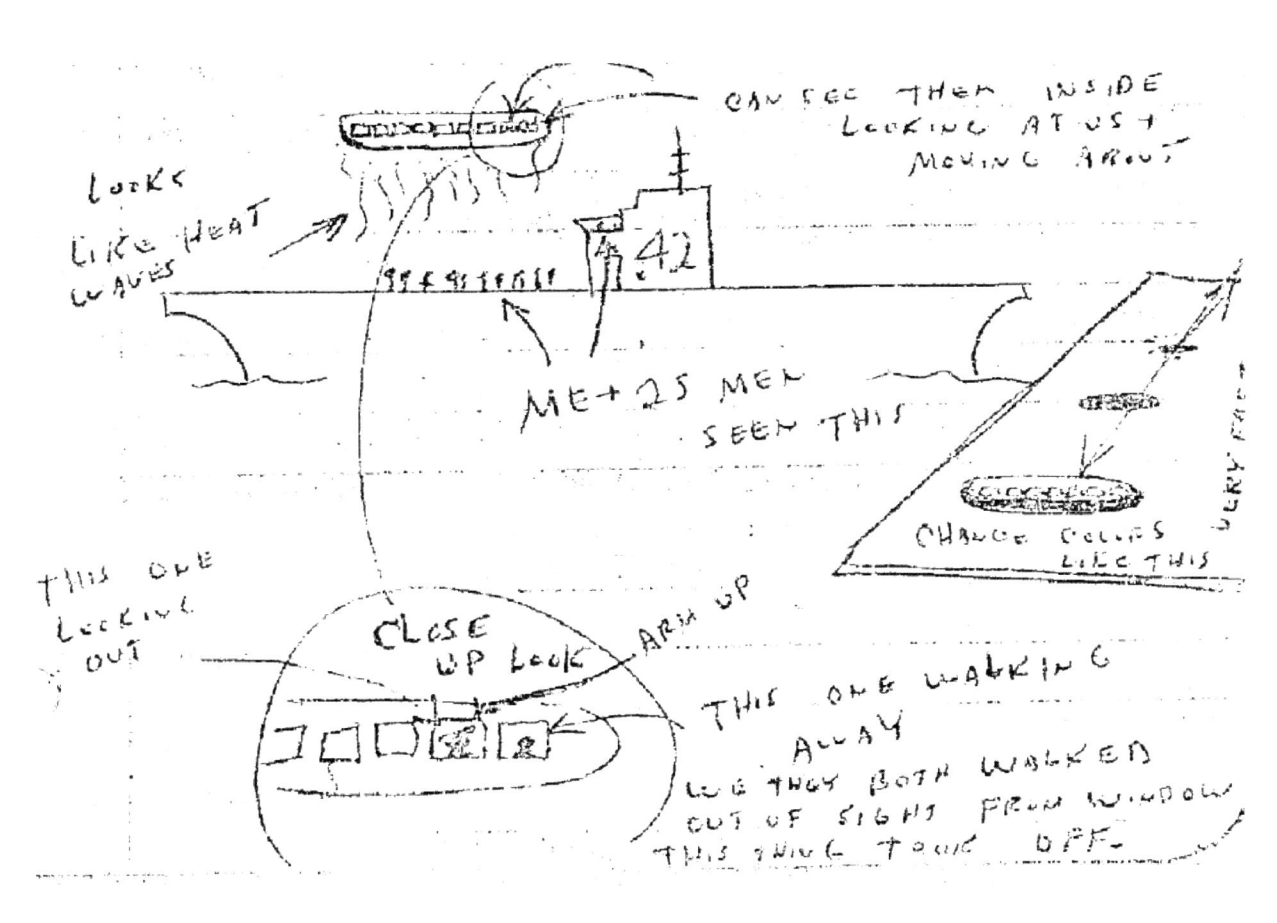

Original MUFON report sketch by Chester Grusinski (US Navy Ret.)

FISHING BOAT CREW SPOTS DIVING UFOS

April 19, 1959, near Japan

APRIL 19, 1959, NEAR JAPAN... ABOARD A FISHING BOAT, THE AMAZED CREW SPOTTED TWO SAUCERS DIVING INTO THE OCEAN AT TERRIFIC SPEED, YET NO WRECKAGE WAS EVER FOUND, AS IF THE UFO'S HAD DELIBERATELY SUBMERGED FOR AN UNDERWATER TRIP.

"THEY WAVED BACK," THE FATHER GILL CASE
June 26, 1959, Papua, New Guinea

It was 6:00 p.m. on the night of June 27, 1959 when Rev. William B. Gill of the Anglican mission at Boianai, Papua, New Guinea had a close encounter he would never forget. That night, he was quickly called out of the mission by Anna Borewa, who was a medical assistant. She excitedly reported strange lights moving towards the settlement. Once outside, Father Gill saw two small UFOs, and a much larger disc-shaped object with four "landing gear" legs protruding from its lower surface. It was hovering over the mission at an altitude of 450 feet, and resembled a two-tiered wedding cake with the lower circular level measuring approximately 35 feet in diameter. The "top deck" was about 20 feet in diameter. Suddenly, four human-looking figures were seen standing on the upper surface of the craft. They appeared to be surrounded by a blue colored light or "aura." Two of them were positioned further back as though they were setting up some type of mechanical equipment.

At this point, there were a total of at least 12 additional witnesses who saw the strange craft hovering in the sky. Then, Father Gill noticed one of the occupants looking down at them, and proceeded to extend his arm above his head in a waving gesture. To his surprise, the figure on the top deck "waved back." Next, Father Gill started flashing a torch at the craft, and after a few minutes, the UFO started making swaying movements apparently in response. Two of the figures went below deck, but returned around 6:30 p.m. and turned on a blue spotlight which they directed skyward. The spotlight was turned on twice for a few seconds each time. At around dusk, the object started moving away, and by 8:00 p.m. was no longer visible. [Sources: CUFOS archives, *International UFO Reporter* November 1977, *Ufology Summer*, 1976, Gray Barker UFO collection.]

Sketch of Father Gill UFO sighting by Elanie Jay

COUNTER ROTATING FLAMING JET UFO

July 13, 1959, Blenheim, New Zealand

It was 5:50 a.m. on the morning of July 13, 1959 when Mrs. Frederick Moreland of Blenheim, New Zealand, was helping her husband tend to their small nine-acre farm. It was still dark out, and there were low clouds covering the area. She had just gone to the barn to start the morning milking of the cows, when she noticed an eerie green glow in the overcast. Then, she saw two large green lights emerge from the clouds, which were rapidly descending towards her direction. She noticed that the entire area was bathed in a green glowing light. Her immediate thought was for her safety, so she made a quick dive for a few trees that were nearby. From the protection of the trees, she got a very close-up and distinct view of a 25-foot diameter flying saucer. The strange craft had two powerful spotlights which were shining down from the underside. The craft was approximately 8 feet in height, and was hovering 15 feet above the ground. It had two rows of "jet" exhaust ports which were located around the outer circumference of the craft. From out of these ports came "orange colored flames" which appeared to be rotating in opposite directions.

Then, the jets stopped, and a light was switched on that illuminated a rectangular, transparent canopy that had a curved top. As the craft was hovering no more than 50 yards away, she could hear a faint "hum" coming from it, and the "air became very warm." At this point, Mrs. Moreland could see two figures inside the curved glass cockpit. They were "dressed in fairly close-fitting suits of shiny material," and they wore "opaque" helmets that came all the way

down to their shoulders. The suits were tight like a wetsuit, and looked like they were made from aluminum foil. A flickering light shone upwards from inside the cockpit, which reflected off their suits. One of the men stood up and put both hands out in front of him as if he were leaning over to look downward. He then emerged from the craft, and walked towards her. Mrs. Moreland stated that the being looked entirely human in appearance. He was about 5-foot, 10-inches tall, and his helmet had a pentagon-shaped glass cut-out window in front. He was wearing a wide belt with a black disc in the center.

He had a harness on his chest that was connected to multiple tubes that led to the bottom of his helmet. Between these tubes, and centered on his chest was a small dial indicator. Interestingly, his left hand appeared to be enclosed in a strange cone or sheath. He shouted at Mrs. Moreland in a foreign language that she could not recognize. He then retreated back to the craft, and sat down. After a few minutes, the jets started up again, and she noticed that the craft began to tilt slightly. Then, it shot up vertically at great speed, and disappeared into the clouds with a *high-pitched whine*. [Sources: "Challenge to Science, The UFO Enigma," Jacques and Janine Valle, 1966 pp24-25, ufoevidence.org, NICAP database. A very comprehensive account of this case can be found at: https://interactives.stuff.co.nz/2018/03/finding-mrs-moreland]

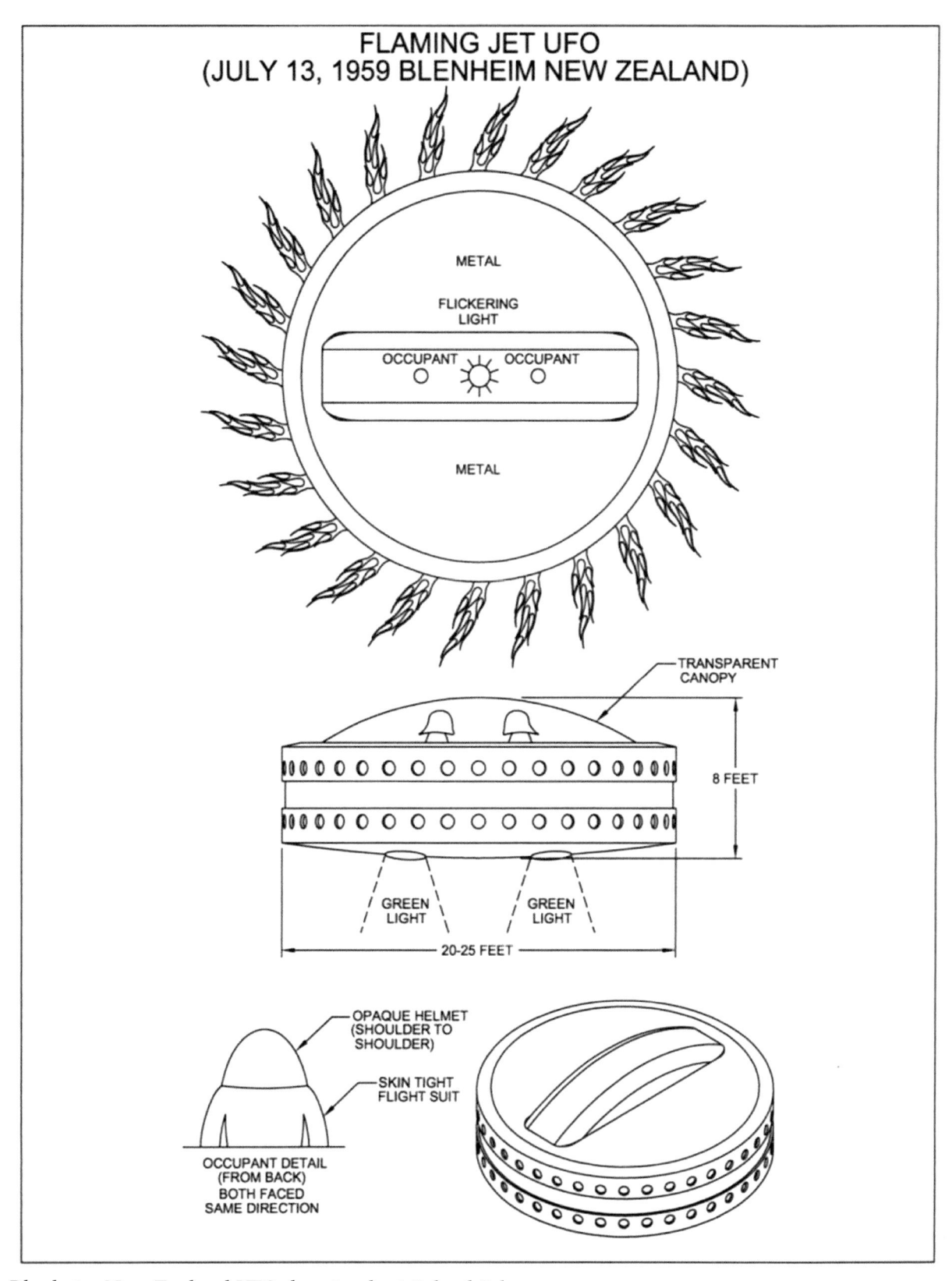

Blenheim New Zealand UFO drawing by Michael Schratt

AUTOMOBILE LEVITATION
1961, Stigler, OK

It was a clear night in 1961 (no exact date given) when Mrs. Maxine Hayes and Mrs. Barbara Lewis were driving their car from Stigler, Oklahoma, on their way home, when they noticed a silver looking object at very close range. As the UFO moved closer, it descended and hovered approximately 12 feet above their vehicle. It resembled a saucer shaped craft, with revolving lights around its outer circumference. Then suddenly, both occupants of the vehicle noticed that their car was being lifted off the road at a height of about 18 inches. The UFO was now pulling their car to the left of the road. Mrs. Hayes reported that she could not do anything to move the vehicle, and the speedometer registered 110 mph. When she took her foot off the accelerator, the car seemed to drop back on the highway. By now, the strange craft was 12 to 18 feet above a few nearby trees. It then moved away at approximately 20 mph, and disappeared near the town of McCurtain. [Sources: *UFO Analysis Report* May-June 1969, *Canadian UFO Report* Vol. 2 No. 6, 1973.]

UNDERWATER MOTORBOAT SURPRISE
June 3, 1961, Savona, Italy

JUNE 3, 1961, SAVONA, ITALY...
GIACOMO BARRA AND HIS COMPANIONS FELT WAVES ROCKING THEIR MOTORBOAT, THEN SAW A HUGE UFO RISE UP OUT OF THE SEA AND SAIL OFF THROUGH THE SKY, AS IF EQUALLY AT HOME IN THE OCEAN OR IN THE AIR.

NAVAL TEST INTERRUPTED
1963, Puerto Rico

During a 1963 naval training exercise off the coast of Puerto Rico, an astonishing event took place. Five U.S. naval vessels were involved, including the USS *Wasp* which served as the "command ship." In addition, two American submarines are believed to have participated as well. Each vessel was linked by way of an advanced electronic communications system. The "strange" event occurred when sonar operator in one of the smaller ships reported to the bridge that one of the submarines had "broken formation," and was in pursuit of an unknown object.

The USO (Unidentified Submerged Object) was travelling at "over 150 knots" (172 mph), and was being tracked by multiple sensors. By comparison, the semi-official record for submerged submarines is 45 knots (51.8 mph), which is held by the U.S. Navy's *Skipjack*. In addition, it was reported that the USO was being monitored for a total of four days, and that it reached depths of up to 27,000 feet. Who had the technology in 1963 to build and operate an underwater craft at such speeds and depths? [Source: "Invisible Residence" by Ivan T. Sanderson]

A SURPRISE VISIT
October 2, 1962, off the coast of Sardinia, west of Italy

On October 2, 1962 (off the coast of Sardinia, west of Italy) a radar operator aboard the carrier USS *Franklin D. Roosevelt* reported a contact 600 miles from the ship at an altitude of 80,000 feet. Shortly thereafter, the unknown object approached the ship at a range of ten miles and 15,000 feet. Then suddenly, the craft began making incredibly sharp angle turns, and was clocked on the ship's radar travelling at a speed of 4,000 mph (no sonic boom was heard). Two F-4 Phantom jets were launched from the deck of the carrier to investigate the unknown craft. Next, the strange object disappeared from the radar screen, only to reappear seconds later. At that point, the UFO approached within a few hundred feet of the ship, and hovered for a few minutes while in full view of multiple crew members.

Records specifically pertaining to this historic case including entries into the ship's logbook were subsequently concealed by official U.S. Navy commanding officers. In fact, during its 32-year commission in active service, the USS *Franklin D. Roosevelt* has been involved in at least six separate incidents involving possible UFOs. One possible explanation for such bazar encounters may be due to the fact that the ship was the first aircraft carrier to be equipped with nuclear weapons on-board. Was an unknown intelligence monitoring our weapons capabilities? [Source: History Channel USS FDR UFO encounters]

THE SOCORRO LANDING
April 24, 1964, Socorro, NM

It was 5:45 p.m., on April 24, 1964 when police officer Lonnie Zamora was chasing a speeding car in Socorro, News Mexico. Suddenly, his attention was drawn away by something he saw in the sky. He had seen a flame from the southwest, and heard a district "roar." Thinking it might be an explosion connected with a nearby building, he gave up the chase and went after the unknown object. As he drove up closer, he could see a light colored "egg-shaped" craft parked on the ground. It was extremely smooth, and was supported by what looked like four slender landing gear legs. The craft measured approximately 12-15 feet long with a strange red colored "insignia" that was centered on its side. The inscription resembled a half circle over an inverted "V," with a vertical line inside, and horizontal line below. It measured 2-1/2 feet high, and two feet wide. Suddenly, officer Zamora was startled to see to small beings wearing white coveralls, standing next to the craft. One of the beings seemed to turn around, and appeared to be looking straight at his squad car.

As he drove closer, a small hill blocked his view of the object. It was at this point, that he heard the sound of a "door closing." When he emerged from the hill, he could no longer see the two beings. He then drove his vehicle as close as the rough terrain would allow, parked,

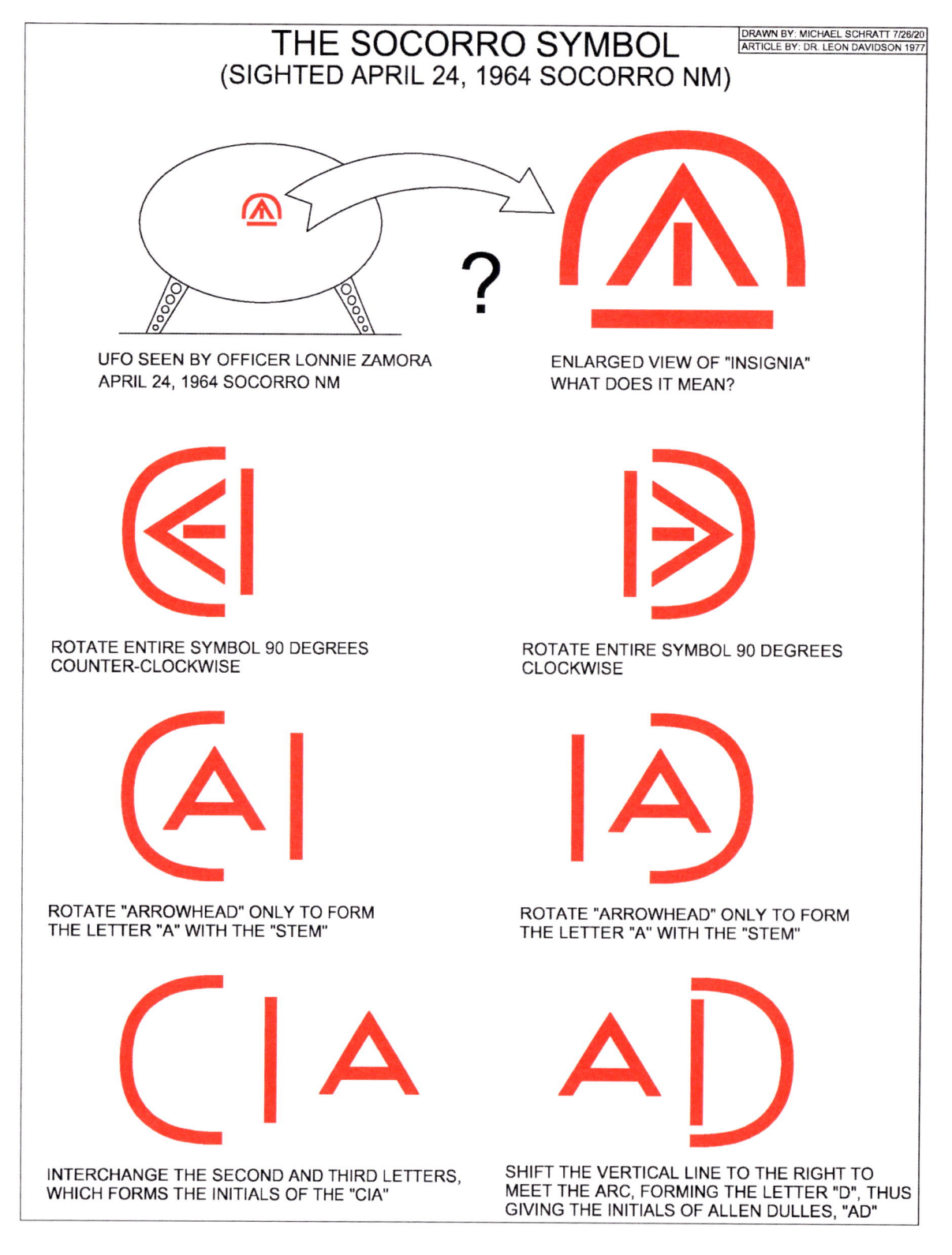

THE SOCORRO SYMBOL
(SIGHTED APRIL 24, 1964 SOCORRO NM)

DRAWN BY: MICHAEL SCHRATT 7/26/20
ARTICLE BY: DR. LEON DAVIDSON 1977

UFO SEEN BY OFFICER LONNIE ZAMORA APRIL 24, 1964 SOCORRO NM

ENLARGED VIEW OF "INSIGNIA" WHAT DOES IT MEAN?

ROTATE ENTIRE SYMBOL 90 DEGREES COUNTER-CLOCKWISE

ROTATE ENTIRE SYMBOL 90 DEGREES CLOCKWISE

ROTATE "ARROWHEAD" ONLY TO FORM THE LETTER "A" WITH THE "STEM"

ROTATE "ARROWHEAD" ONLY TO FORM THE LETTER "A" WITH THE "STEM"

INTERCHANGE THE SECOND AND THIRD LETTERS, WHICH FORMS THE INITIALS OF THE "CIA"

SHIFT THE VERTICAL LINE TO THE RIGHT TO MEET THE ARC, FORMING THE LETTER "D", THUS GIVING THE INITIALS OF ALLEN DULLES, "AD"

Author's special note: Why was the so called fake "umbrella" symbol (shown above) actively promoted by USAF Captain Richard T. Holder?

and then got out. At this point, he heard two or three loud "thumps," as though someone was hammering, or shutting a door. These occurred approximately one second apart. As he started walking towards the object, it began to roar. The strange sound began at a low frequency, but soon quickly rose to a higher frequency in just a few seconds. He also saw blue-colored flames exiting the bottom of the craft. Assuming that the object was about to explode, he quickly jumped behind his vehicle. Then, the roaring sound stopped, and he could see the craft hovering silently a few feet above the ground. The UFO then moved away slowly, and gathered speed as it headed towards a nearby dynamite shack. Source: "Unidentified Flying Objects Briefing Document, The Best Available Evidence", December 1995. [Reference: "Not of this World, The 1964 Socorro UFO Humanoids: Witness, Policeman Lonnie Zamora", by Ben Moss 2020.]

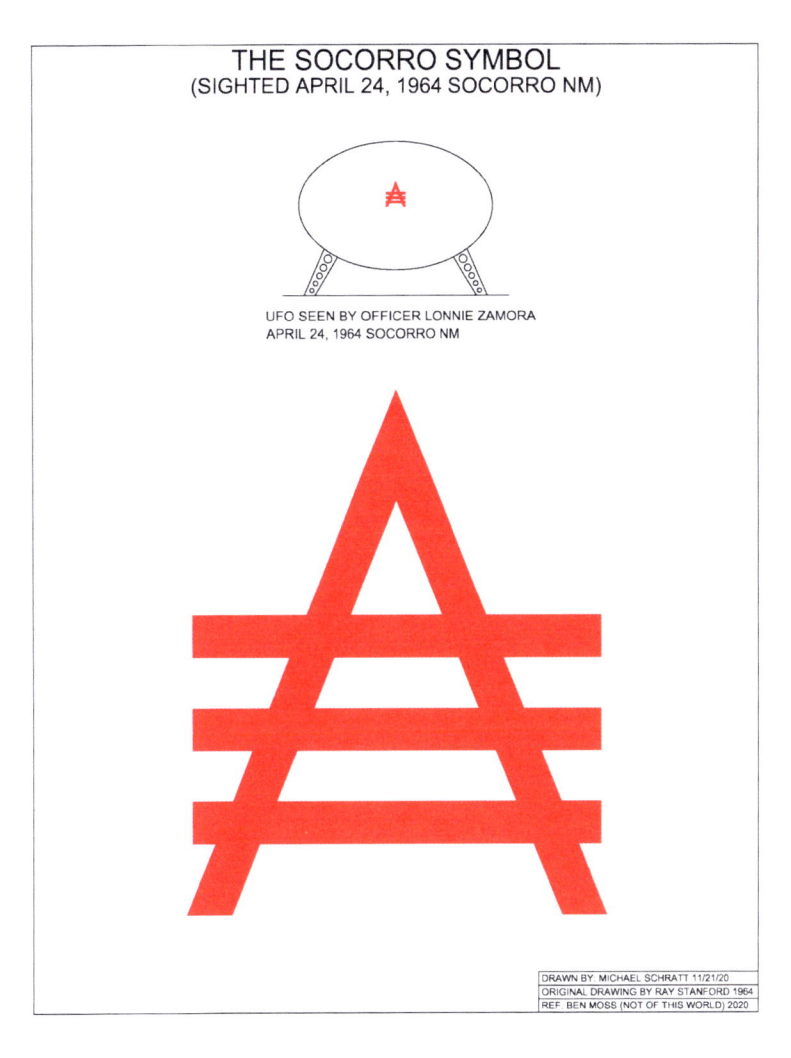

[The authentic/corrected Symbol as per Ray Stanford (April 1964).

"FLAMING TOP" UFO
June 29, 1964, Lavonia, GA

On the night of June 29, 1964, businessman Beauford E. Parham was driving home near Lavonia, Georgia, when he spotted a bright light heading directly towards his vehicle. Suddenly the strange light moved directly in front of his headlights even though he was moving at a speed of 65 mph. Mr. Parham could see the appearance of a "top shaped" object which emitted an unusual sound similar to the "hissing of many snakes." The craft was amber colored in appearance, and it was spinning along its vertical axis. It measured approximately 6 feet high, and 8 feet wide. The UFO also had a mast-like protrusion on top, with port holes running along the mid-section of the outer circumference. Flames were visible exiting each port-hole as the craft rotated.

The unknown object disappeared briefly, only to return again directly of his vehicle while moving at a speed of 65 mph. Then, it went over his car, leaving a gaseous vapor in its wake. Finally, the strange craft appeared for a third time in front of his car which now began to sputter, and eventually, Mr. Parham pulled over and stopped. The object then began to rotate more quickly, and disappeared in a "split second." An oily substance remained on the vehicle after subsequent attempts to wash it off. In addition, the vehicle's hood was clearly warped, with significant paint deterioration. Post examination of the vehicle by Federal Aviation Administration (FAA) officials at a nearby air-base found slight traces of radiation, thereby putting this sighting into the category of a CEII. [Sources: NICAP, "Uninvited Guests" by Richard Hall.]

"BEEHIVE" UFO ENCOUNTER
December 21, 1964, Fishersville, VA

DEC. 21, 1964, FISHERSVILLE, VA.... WHILE DRIVING, HORACE BURNS SAW A GIANT UFO, SHAPED LIKE A BEEHIVE WITH A DOME ON TOP, MEASURING 125 FEET IN DIAMETER AND 80 TO 90 FEET HIGH. HE SAW IT LAND FOR A WHILE THEN FLY AWAY.

A MOST CURIOUS MORNING COMMUTE

March 23, 1966, Temple, OK

It was 5:05 a.m. on the morning of March 23, 1966 when Eddie Laxson (56-year-old electronics instructor from Sheppard Air Force Base of Wichita Falls, in Wichita County, Texas), was travelling west on highway 70 near the Texas/Oklahoma boarder. Suddenly, his headlights illuminated a strange object that was blocking the road ahead. Mr. Laxson stopped his car, got out, and observed what looked like a "fish"-shaped craft. It measured approximately 75 feet in length, eight feet high, and 12 feet wide. It was sitting on what looked like retractable landing gear legs. There was a 3-foot diameter transparent "bubble canopy" at the extreme front end of the craft, and it appeared to be lit from inside. Two powerful "headlights" attached to the top lit up the surrounding area. It also had aft facing lights, as well. The unknown craft looked very smooth in appearance, and was completely devoid of any major seams, rivets or fasteners.

It had no apparent wings or any visible means of propulsion. The object had a shiny aluminum exterior finish. There also appeared to be very small "control surfaces" which were located near its aft end. On its upper surface, it had a curved "spire" or "stinger" which swept back at a 45-degree angle towards the rear. This protrusion was connected to a small "knob" at the end which resembled a baseball. This strange apparatus looked very similar to the "pole" that protrudes up from the top of an electric trolley car. Mr. Laxson could also see a 3-foot diameter "porthole" window that was divided into four equal pie segments. Just aft of this window, he could see letters written in black paint that read "TL4768." These were positioned vertically on the side of the craft. Mr. Laxson wasn't entirely sure about the last two characters, but that was his closest estimation.

Near the front of the object, he could see a "doorway" that opened outwards forming stairs that led to the ground. It measured about 4 feet tall, and 2-1/2 feet wide. Near this doorway, he spotted a man who was shining a flashlight towards the bottom of the vehicle. He was dressed in green military Air Force fatigue-style coveralls, and was wearing a baseball cap with the bill turned up. On his upper sleeves, Mr. Laxson could see what looked like military type rank "chevron" symbols on the unidentified man. He appeared to be about 30 years old. Suddenly, as if being noticed by the intruder, the mysterious man quickly climbed the ladder of the craft, and shut the door. Then, Mr. Laxson recalled hearing a *high-pitched drilling noise.* He could also hear the sound like that of a welding rod when an arc is struck. Incredibly, the craft rose approximately 50 feet above the ground, and then darted away at a speed estimated to be approximately 720 mph. There was no sonic boom heard during its rapid departure.

After the object disappeared, Mr. Laxson got back into his car drove approximately 15 miles down the highway. He later stopped and talked with another individual who had also stopped to watch a few lights over the Red River six miles to the southeast. Additional reports indicated that truck drivers saw similar objects along the same stretch of road. The case was officially investigated by Project Blue Book investigators and was listed as an "unknown." [Sources: U.S. Air Force Project Blue Book, CUFOS archives, Gray Barker historical UFO archives, David Marler historical UFO archives, *The Interplanetary Intelligence Report*, May-June 1966, *The Lawton Constitution* March 25, 1966.]

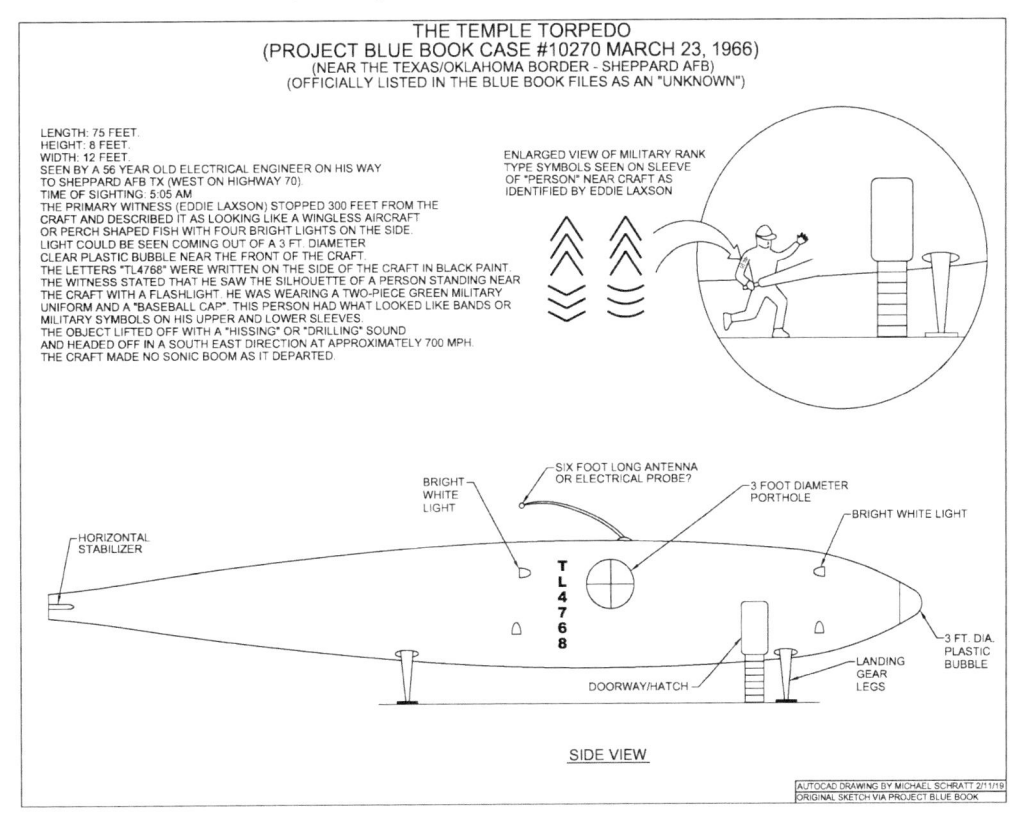

Drawing by Michael Schratt

RECESS INTERUPTED
April 6, 1966 Melbourne, Australia

On April 6, 1966 something very strange happened at Westall High School in Clayton, Australia, (a suburb of Melbourne). A small group of High School students witnessed a silver-colored flying saucer pass directly over the schoolyard. It was about 16 feet across with a small dark-colored dome on top. Moments later, multiple terrified students rushed inside and were screaming to gct the attention of their fellow students and teachers. At that point, the school bell rang, signaling the time for recess. Both excited and scared, at least 200 students poured out of the school in time to witness the strange spectacle. In addition, adult staff members of the school also saw the strange craft, as well. In a hurried rush, the school's chemistry teacher picked up a camera and snapped multiple photographs of the saucer and the panicked students. The UFO appeared to be flying next to a group of nearby power lines. It could hover, and dart away at incredible speeds. Multiple students confirmed that they also saw a group of small general aviation light planes circling around the saucer in an apparent effort to get a better view. Once the UFO "noticed" it was being chased by the planes, it quickly sped off.

At this point, a group of students climbed over a perimeter fence and headed off to wooded area known as the "The Grange," where one of the craft appeared to have landed. Two girls were ahead of the rest of the group, and arrived near where the saucer came down. Apparently, one

Excited students climb a nearby fence to get a better view of the two landed UFOs.

One Westall student apparently had a very close encounter which left her traumatized

of these students had a very "close encounter" with the UFO, and it is believed that she came within a few feet of the craft. By the time the rest of the students arrived, they could see the craft rise above the trees, and fly off. They also noticed a discolored circular "burnt patch" left over from where the craft was believed to have touched down. Shaken, terrified, and traumatized, the student that had reached the scene first in the woods, was taken away by an ambulance, and was never seen or heard from again. An additional witness who confirmed the sighting claimed he saw two flying saucers land near his vicinity before it was seen by the students in The Grange.

The two craft he saw had no rivets, seams or fasteners of any kind, and looked like it was manufactured in one solid piece from a mold. They were sitting on the ground approximately nine feet apart, and when he walked toward one of the discs, he could feel "heat" rising from its surface. By now, an additional group of students overcome by curiosity jumped a small fence to examine the strange unknown machines. Within a few minutes, both craft slowly rose off the ground, and flew away. When the students returned to school, they were called to a large assembly room by the headmaster, and were told not to discuss the event. Eventually, additional men in suits and military personnel arrived at the school and pressured the students into silence. [Sources: *The Dandenong Journal* April 14, 1966, Westall 66, *A Suburban UFO mystery*, Documentary film by Rosie Jones can be found at: https://www.youtube.com/watch?v=sAAXF2mbfjA]

"STOP THE PRESS"
October 26, 1966

OCT. 26, 1966, 5:00 P.M....
AS REPORTED BY MRS. C. PARKINS
OF FORT WAYNE, IND., A STRANGE "FOOTBALL"
HOVERED OVER A NEWSPAPER PLANT, WHOSE STACKING
MACHINERY WENT TEMPORARILY OUT-OF-ORDER, AS
IF AN "EM EFFECT" (ELECTROMAGNETIC RAY) CAME
FROM THE UFO.

"TIC-TAC" UAP ENCOUNTER
March 1967, Wycombe, PA

Illustration by Michel Schratt

Since the *New York Times* published its famous December 16, 2017 article on "Tic-Tac" shaped UAP sighted by U.S. Navy pilots, there has been a renewed interest by the general public in this phenomenon. According the article, during November of 2004, Commander David Fravor, and Commander Jim Slaight were on a training mission approximately 100 of the coast of San Diego. They were flying F-18F Super Hornets which originated from the USS *Nimitz*. Suddenly, both pilots were alerted to something that was being tracked on radar by the USS *Princeton* at an altitude of 80,000 feet. The strange craft then descended to 20,000 feet and began to hover. Next, Commander Fravor looked down, and could see an "oval" or "tic-tac" shaped craft hovering approximately 50 feet above the water. It measured approximately 40 feet long, and had no wings, tail, control surfaces or any visible means of propulsion. Commander Fravor then descended to get a closer look, and noticed that the strange craft was now ascending towards him. Soon thereafter, the craft accelerated "like nothing he had ever seen." The high-definition camera on-board the F/A-18F recorded video footage of a strange "oval" shaped object that had hook shaped

VINTAGE STEAM "BOILER" UFO
(SIGHTED MARCH 1967, WYCOMBE PA.)

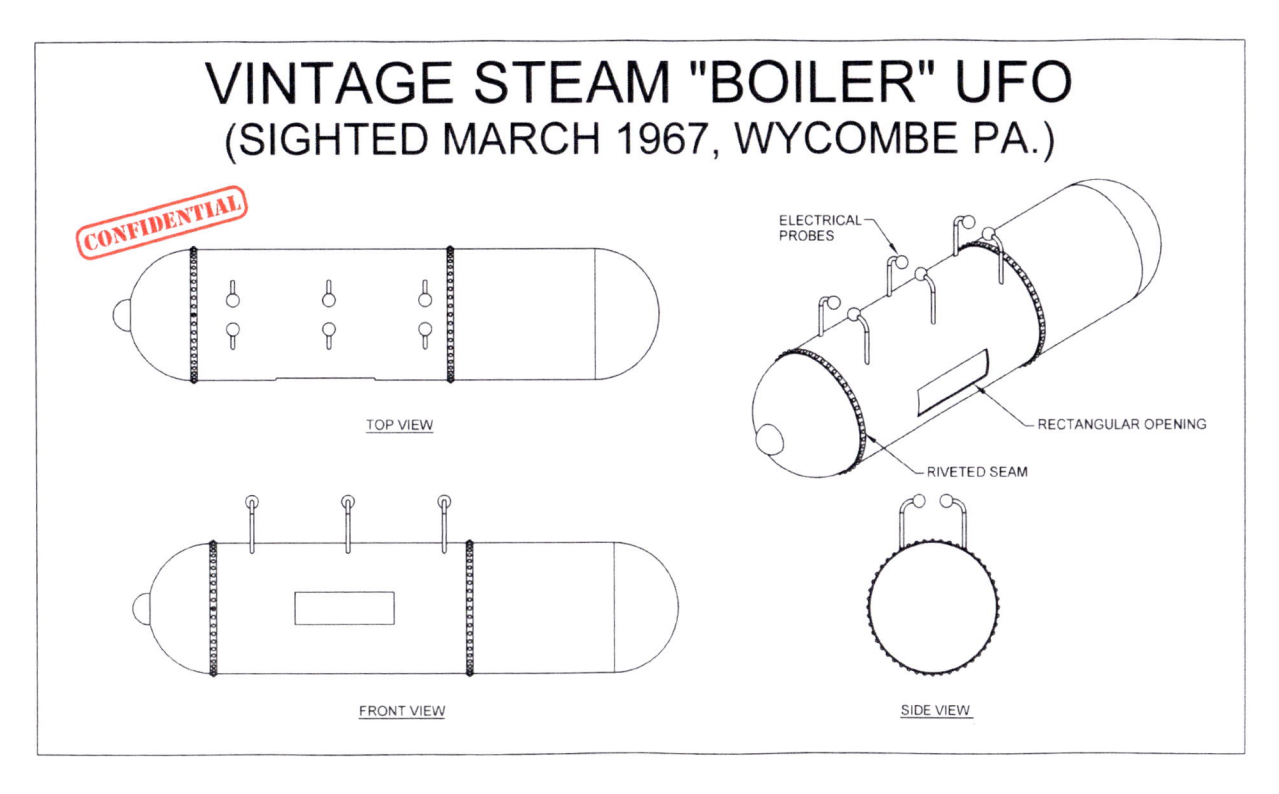

"Tic-Tac" shaped UFO with "prongs" seen in Wycombe PA. March 1967. Drawing by Michael Schratt

"prongs or protrusions" rising off its surface. What purpose did these strange appendages serve, and were they directly related to its propulsion system?

It is interesting to note that sightings of so called "tic-tac" or "cough-drop" shaped UFOs are not an isolated incident, and reports of these craft date back long <u>BEFORE</u> the USS *Nimitz* encounter of 2004. During March of 1967, a "tic-tac" UFO was witnessed in daylight hovering over Wycombe, Pennsylvania. It closely resembled the outer shape and size of the craft seen by the two Navy pilots *37 years later*. In addition, the 1967 craft also had the "prongs or protrusions" rising of its surface (as seen in the 2004 high-definition footage). Also, the witness of the Wycombe tic-tac reported seeing "riveted seams" which clearly point to a man-made origin. Are these strange features part of a "spark gap" electrical discharge device closely associated with a high voltage power source? This author has 12 additional cases of UFO sightings which include prongs, protrusions, hooks, "stingers" and "spires" emanated off the surface of these strange craft.

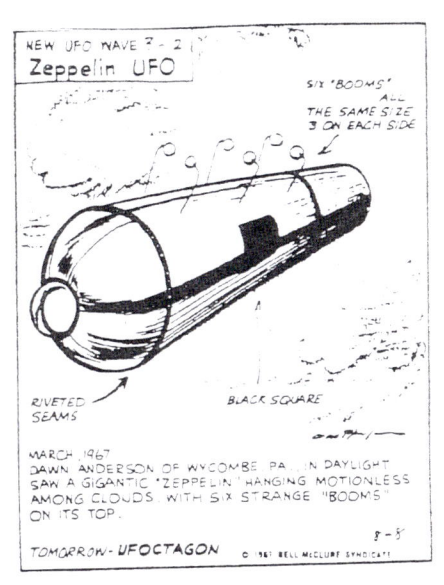

Sketch of "Tic-Tac" shaped UFO by Carl Pfeufer via Otto Binder (Our Space Age 1965-1969)

WEEKEND PROSPECTING INTERRUPTED
May 19, 1967, Falcon Lake, Manitoba, Canada

It was May 20, 1967, when Stephen Michalak from Winnipeg was prospecting near Falcon Lake, Manitoba, Canada. At the time of the incident, he was wearing thick leather gloves, and a welder's mask to protect his eyes from rock chips. As he was examining a rock formation, Mr. Michalak noticed two flying saucers which were hovering above him. One remained in the immediate area for a few moments, but then quickly departed at a high rate of speed. The other craft landed approximately 200 feet from his location. As he walked closer to the craft, he described it as being approximately 40 feet in diameter and 10 feet tall. It had a 10-foot diameter dome on top with a flat roof. Running along the outer circumference of the lower dome section, there appeared to be two rows of elongated "slits." The craft had a highly-polished "chrome" appearance that almost looked like "liquid Mercury." The strange object had no visible seams, joints or rivets, and looked as though it was machined out of one solid block of aluminum. It had no identifying markings, and Stephen initially thought that this might be an *experimental craft originating from the United States*.

As he walked closer, a 2-foot X 3-foot door or hatch opened, which emitted a strange violet/purple colored light. He could also see a much smaller (6-inch X 8-inch) "exhaust vent" which was located just to the left of the hatch. The exhaust vent was composed of 30 perfectly spaced drilled holes that looked like they were made with high precision machinery. At this point, he was standing no more than 3 feet from the craft. Next, he looked inside the hatch, but was blinded by the bright light, and had to lower his visor to protect his eyes. He could hear

Stephen Michalak examines the interior of the strange craft and attempts communication

unintelligible voices coming from inside, and even tried communicating with whoever might be in the craft by using English, Russian, German, French, and Italian. Immediately thereafter, the hatch slammed shut, and he noticed a high-pitched whining noise. Next, he reached out his hand and actually touched the craft, and was instantly burned despite wearing gloves. Then, the craft lifted a few inches off the ground, and started to rotate counter-clockwise.

At that point, the "exhaust vent" eventually lined up with where he was standing, and the "gases" burned his cap, outer and inner garments, and he sustained severe stomach and chest burns. Disoriented and in pain, Stephen staggered back to Winnipeg after a grueling nine-hour walk. He underwent several medical examinations after the incident, and developed strange first-degree burn marks on his chest. These marks were comparable to a silver dollar in size, and matched the exact hole pattern of the "exhaust vent" on the strange craft. Soil samples taken by Mr. Michalak from the immediate area occupied by the UFO were analyzed and found to be radioactive, making this one of the top CEII cases in all of UFOlogy. The case was investigated by the RCMP (Royal Canadian Mounted Police), which could provide no evidence that would dispute Mr. Michalak's account. [Sources: "Unidentified Flying Objects Briefing Document, The Best Available Evidence" by Don Berliner and Antonio Huneeus December 1995, *UFO Analysis Report*, May-June 1968, Gray Barker UFO collection (Clarksburg WV).]

Enlarged view, note 20" wall thickness and violet/purple colored light.

Note "elongated slots" located on lower surface of upper dome

Note how "hole pitch" of "exhaust vent" precisely lines up with burn marks on Mr. Michalak's chest

Official photograph of the Falcon Lake UFO landing site taken by the RCMP. Note outline of ring where bottom of craft contacted the ground

A MOST INTERESTING FISHING TRIP

May 1967, Hartwell Lake, Anderson, SC

MAY, 1967...
MR. X. (NAME WITHHELD BY REQUEST) OF ANDERSON, S.C., WAS FISHING ON HARTWELL LAKE AND SAW AN OCTAGONAL UFO APPARENTLY PUMPING UP WATER THROUGH A METAL TUBE. MR. X. WAS NEAR ENOUGH TO CAST AND STRIKE THE OBJECT, BUT NOBODY CAME OUT AND IT SOON SHOT AWAY INTO THE SKY.

"FAT FRISBEE" OVER DETROIT
July 1967

THE DETROIT DISC
(SIGHTED JULY 1967, NEAR DETROIT)

RESTRICTED

REVOLVING BAND OF LIGHTS

100 FEET IN DIA.
SIDE VIEW

During the summer of 1967, Tom P. and Jim H. (last names on file in the author's personal archives) witnessed a strange craft hovering over Redford Township, a suburb of Detroit, Michigan. The time was 9:30 p.m., and the weather was clear. Both witnesses described seeing saucer shaped craft that measured approximately 100 feet in diameter, and 30 feet thick. The object had band of lights which were revolving clockwise about its vertical axis. The sighting lasted about two minutes, and the craft departed at an incredible speed without a sound. [Source: CUFOS archives]

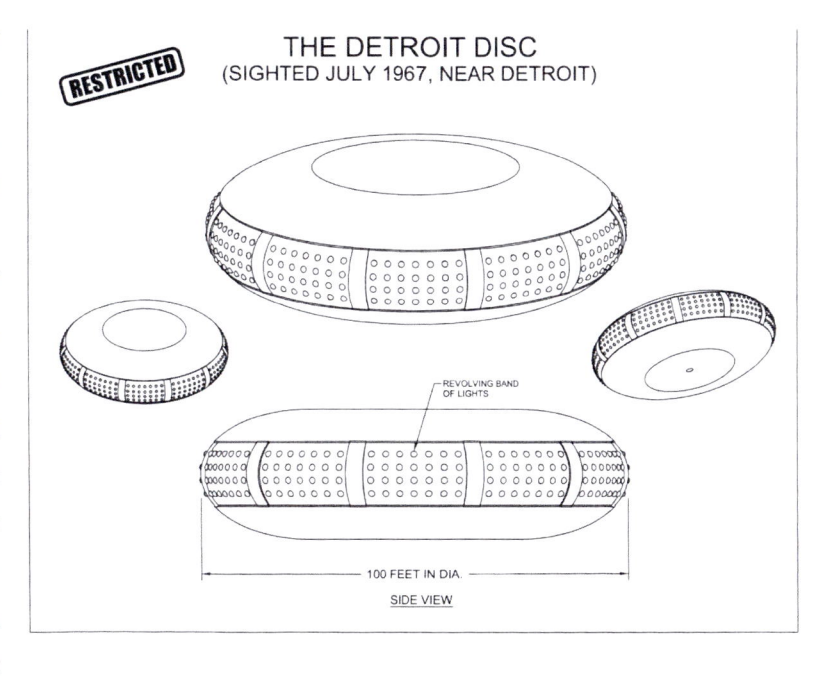

THE EMERGING TURQUOISE BALL
August 4, 1967, Gulf north of Arrecife, Venezuela

On August 4, 1967 Dr. Hugo Yepez was fishing in a gulf of north Arrecife, Venezuela when he noticed that the water began to boil in a circle measuring eighteen feet in diameter. Then, he witnessed a gray/blue globe emerge from the surface and hover nearby. The strange object had water dripping off its exterior, and was described as having a "revolving section with triangular windows." It then shot upwards into space. Source: *The UFO Investigator* Vol. IV No. 5 March 1968

THE CHAOTIC CASE OF THE "VENT UFO"
August 1967

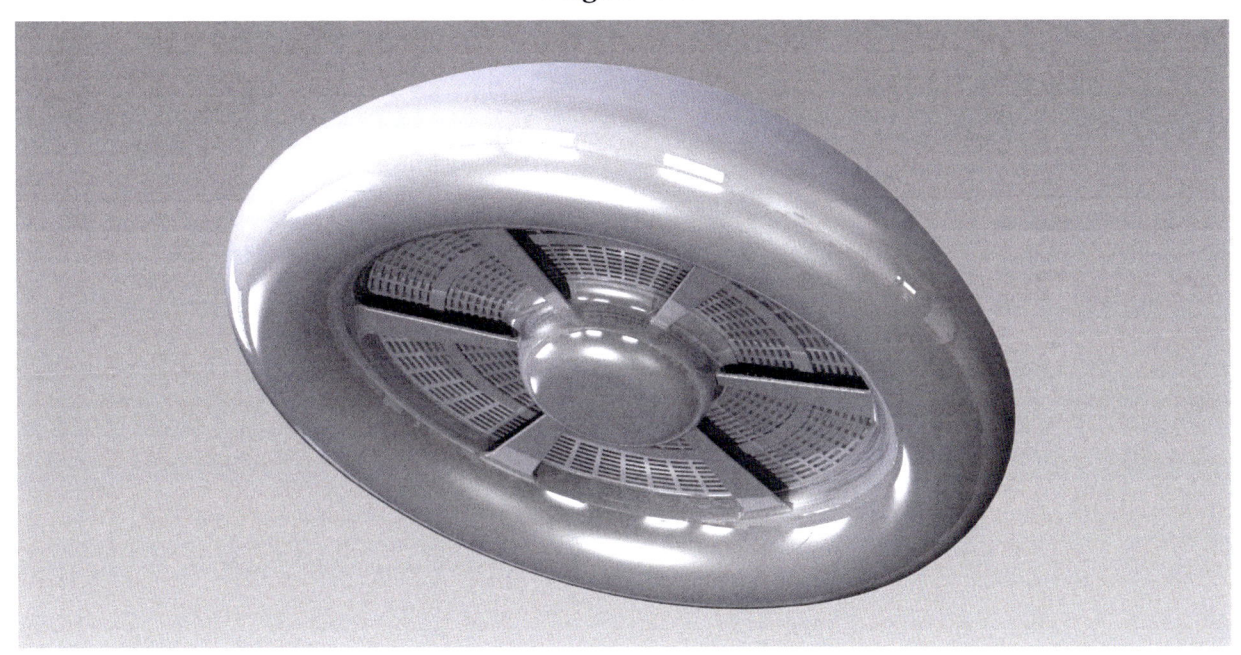

During August of 1967, (exact date unknown) a Calgary area chiropractor was riding his horse near the Sarcee Indian Reservation in Canada. Suddenly, his horse became nervous, and started violently twisting and turning. Then, the doctor noticed a strange low flying cloud ahead that was approximately 70 feet across. Seconds later, a solid object slowly emerged which appeared to be about 40 feet in diameter. The chiropractor stated that the craft was made of a material that looked like plastic or fiberglass. The bottom of the UFO resembled a mushroom, and it had silvery blue color.

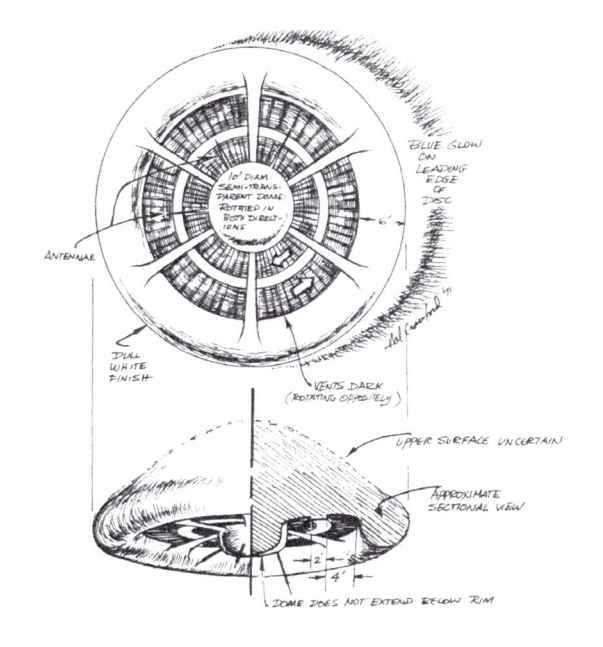

There appeared to be two concentric circular vent-like structures on its lower surface which were rotating in opposite directions. These were separated by a circular casing which was about 2 feet wide. The lower surface also contained a 10-foot diameter dome which had tapering beams connected to the outer rim. A brilliant electric blue light which looked like a "welder's arc" was visible along the leading edge of the craft. Within a few minutes, the unusual object returned to its cloud, and departed to the southwest. [Source: *Canadian UFO Report* issue No. 1-2 (Spring 1971).]

GLOBE SHAPED UFO WITH TRANSPARENT DOME

January 24, 1968, Indiana, PA

JAN. 24, 1968... AT INDIANA, PENNSYLVANIA, A WITNESS SAW A SAUCER HOVERING OVER A POND, WITH TWO OCCUPANTS WHO WERE APPARENTLY REPAIRING THEIR EQUIPMENT.

THE "FLAMING SKULL" UFO
May 6, 1968, Elyria, OH

MAY 6, 1968, 10:30 P.M..... CAMPING OUT WITH A FRIEND, JOSEPH PLASO OF ELYRIA, OHIO, SAW AN AMAZING SKULL-SHAPED UFO SURROUNDED BY FLAMES, WHICH FLASHED DOWN AN INTENSE SEARCHLIGHT BEAM FOR SEVERAL MINUTES BEFORE FLYING AWAY.

"MICHELIN MAN" ENCOUNTER
July 31, 1968, Reunion Island

On July 31, 1968 M. Luce Fontaine, age 31, was picking grass for his rabbits on France's Reunion Island in the Indian Ocean when he came across something truly incredible. He had bent down momentarily, and then saw a strange object sitting on the ground no more than 80 feet from him. It had an elliptical/oval or "egg shape" shape, and was suspended off the ground approximately 13 feet. The strange craft measured 16 feet across. The forward part facing him had a transparent section, while both extremities were opaque dark blue in color. The craft featured a supporting wide base which tapered as it rose upward. This section resembled shiny metal. There was an identical base located on the top.

In the center of the craft were two individuals, with their backs towards him. The one on the left turned around, and faced Mr. Fontaine. It measured approximately 35 inches tall, and was wearing what looked like an inflatable ribbed diving suit. The strange being closely resembled the so called "Michelin Man." The being on the right simply turned his head which was partially concealed by a fully enclosed helmet that featured a small rectangular transparent section. Suddenly, both turned their backs, and there was a brilliant flash of light similar to that given off by an arc welder. At that exact moment, everything appeared totally white all around him. Mr. Fontaine also felt an intense heat from the craft, and a powered blast of wind. When local officials investigated the case, they found residual amounts of radiation on the ground where the craft had been sitting, and also on the clothes of Mr. Fontaine. [Source: *Flying Saucer Review* January/February 1969]

HELICOPTER SURPRISE
September 9, 1968, Dong Ha, Viet Nam

SEP. 9, 1968, DONG HA, VIET NAM

A HELICOPTER CREW OF THE U.S. KNEW IT WAS NO VIET CONG CRAFT THAT MADE FANTASTIC MANEUVERS THROUGH THE SKY FOR 20 MINUTES, BUT WAS A GENUINE UFO.

CHILLY ENCOUNTER ON THE SLOPES
January 7, 1970, Heinola, Finland

It was 2:45 p.m. on January 7, 1970 when Aaron Heinonen and Esko Viljo were skiing 16 kilometers northeast of the town of Heinola in Finland. They headed in the direction of a small slope to take a break. A few minutes later, a strange cloud approached them from the north. Then, it made a wide sweeping turn, and approached them from the south. The cloud emitted a powerful light, and made a "whirring" sound. The light turned into a pulsating, red-colored fog, and bursts of smoke could be seen emanating from its top surface. The cloud then descended towards them, and stopped at an altitude of 50 feet above the ground. At that point, they could both see the outline of a strange, round, metallic craft that was embedded inside. It was 10 feet in diameter, with a dome on top. The bottom consisted of 3 equally spaced, half-hemispherical globes, which were protruding down. There also appeared to be a small ring or tube on the bottom

The craft was so close they could have touched it with their ski poles. A strong beam of light emanated from the lower surface of the craft which blinded both men. The beam moved around on the ground before it stopped and formed a shining circle on the snow below. At that point, a light, reddish-colored gray fog encompassed the immediate surrounding area. The cone of light started to be "sucked" into the craft and had ascended half a meter, when the men saw a black disc which measured 15 cm in diameter. The strange black disc remained suspended in the air momentarily, and with a "ticking sound," the disc disappeared into the tube on the underside of the craft.

It was at this point, that both men noticed something truly fantastic. Standing in front of them was what could be best described as a small "garden gnome." It measured approximately 3 feet high, and was wearing a tight-fitting green coverall with darker colored green boots, and white gloves that reached its elbows. Its face had a very aged and deeply "wrinkled" look, and its body had a very slender build. The small being had the arms of a very skinny child, and it had a st[...] were very claw like in appearan[ce...] appearance. The strange being wa[s holding] a camera.

The creature pointed the "camera" at both men like it was

Drawing by Kent Nillson

taking pictures. A dense reddish gray fog descended from the craft, and large sparks emanated out from the cone of light in which the creature was standing. Suddenly, the fog became denser obscuring the view of the entity. Then, the cone of light converged, and appeared to retract back into the bottom of the craft. At that point, the veil of mist dissipated, and the craft disappeared. In a state of shock both men stood motionless and didn't speak for at least 3 minutes as they were trying to assess the situation. Aaron felt his right foot become numb, and he was forced to leave his skis on the site and be led home by Esko. Upon arriving home, Aaron got a severe headache and his back was hurting. He also had difficulty breathing and started to vomit, qualifying this as one of the most significant CEII cases in UFOlogy. [Sources: CUFOS, Gray Barker UFO collection.]

THE FLYING IRON
October 9, 1972, Long Island, NY

It was 7:30 p.m. on October 9, 1972 when a couple was driving down a lonely stretch of road between Smithtown and Coram, Long Island, New York. They had just left their home in Smithtown and were running an errand in Coram. Driving east, they had reached the midpoint of their trip, when they both noticed a bright white light that resembled the landing light on an airplane. They drove several more blocks, and noticed that the light did not appear to be moving. Then, the wife noticed that the strange light was approaching them. With their attention fixated on the object, they both observed red and green lights attached to the object. The larger white light appeared to be pulsating like a "heartbeat." At this point, the object disappeared from view as they approached a small hill between Seldon and Coram. Midway along the dark and deserted stretch of highway, the light suddenly came back into view above the treetops.

The wife looked up and reported that she was directly under the belly of a strange craft. She yelled to her husband to pull off the side of the road and stop the car. It was clear at this point that they were both observing something other than an aircraft. The wife jumped out of their vehicle to get a better view. Despite his own fascination with the object, the husband admitted that he did not exit the vehicle himself, because he was parked on a very narrow shoulder. Staying in the car, the husband rolled down the window and leaned his head out to get a better view. Both eyewitnesses agreed that what they observed looked like an elongated ellipse with a single row of lights (five or six) running along the bottom surface on both sides. Watching the UFO from a nearby embankment, the wife observed several features on the craft that the husband could not from his perspective in the car. The craft was dark in color, and was triangular in shape with a rounded front end, and squared off back.

As the object passed overhead, she observed two vertical "antennas" or poles sticking up from the top surface of the craft near its aft end. These poles tapered in diameter as they rose vertically. Stretching between the two poles, she could see a thin "wire." These features gave the craft a very "homemade" appearance as though someone had "made it in their garage." After a few minutes, the craft slowly departed that area. [Source: *UFO Investigator* February 1972.]

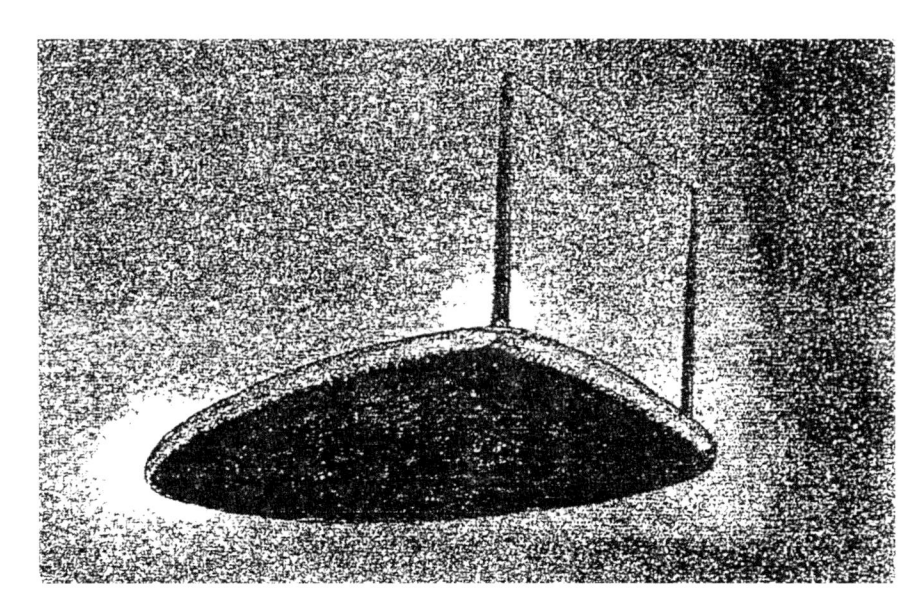

Primary eyewitness sketch of the "flying platform" he and his wife observed in 1972.

"THE FLAMING ELLIPSE"
December 26, 1972, Maracaibo, Venezuela

It was approximately 8:00 p.m. on the night of December 26, 1972, when "RS" (actual name on on file in the author's personal archives) was with his wife and daughter on the top floor of their apartment complex in Maracaibo, Venezuela. The primary eyewitness and his wife had just stepped out onto the balcony, and were looking for a plane (a Convair) that usually came in low over the buildings during most evenings. The weather was clear, and visibility was unlimited. They were facing northeast, expecting to see the aircraft, when they saw a strange object approaching them that was approximately 3 miles away. The object gave the appearance of an aircraft engine fire that was flaming from the lower half of a nacelle, under a wing. The primary eyewitness stated that he tried to spot an aircraft to go along with the fire, but at that exact moment, the craft turned and pulled up to miss the tops of some nearby buildings. It was at this point, that he could see this was no type of conventional aircraft.

After passing two small buildings, it changed direction to its original flight path. The craft then descended just below their observation level, and passed within 150 feet from where they were standing. Both husband and wife got a very distinct, clear view of the craft. Its shape was somewhat elliptical, with a rounded front end, and tapering sides that ended with an abruptly squared-off stern. It was approximately 50 feet in length, and 40 feet wide. Attached beneath the vehicle and slightly forward of the center, were two large (36-inch diameter) opposed hemispherical type "insulators." Each insulator contained one opposing "electrode" that appeared to be about 7 inches in diameter with a "gap" of about 5 inches between them. Between these two "electrodes" was a full, complete and continuous "electric" arc similar to a carbon arc lamp or a welder's stinger. Small wisps of smoke came off this arc which travelled along with the craft rather than dissipate by the wind. This arc illuminated the underside of the vehicle in fine detail.

The object then headed towards the local airport about 15 miles away. At the airport, the craft made multiple, smooth level turns, and followed the contour of the airfield. It then changed direction, and continued on its original course until it disappeared approximately 30 miles away. Moments after the first vehicle was no longer visible, both eyewitnesses were looking in the direction of the airport when they glanced up, and were startled to see a *second vehicle* travelling on the same flight path as the first craft. This one was moving very slowly (about 10 mph) and was about 350 feet above both witnesses. At this point, "RS" asked his daughter to borrow a pair

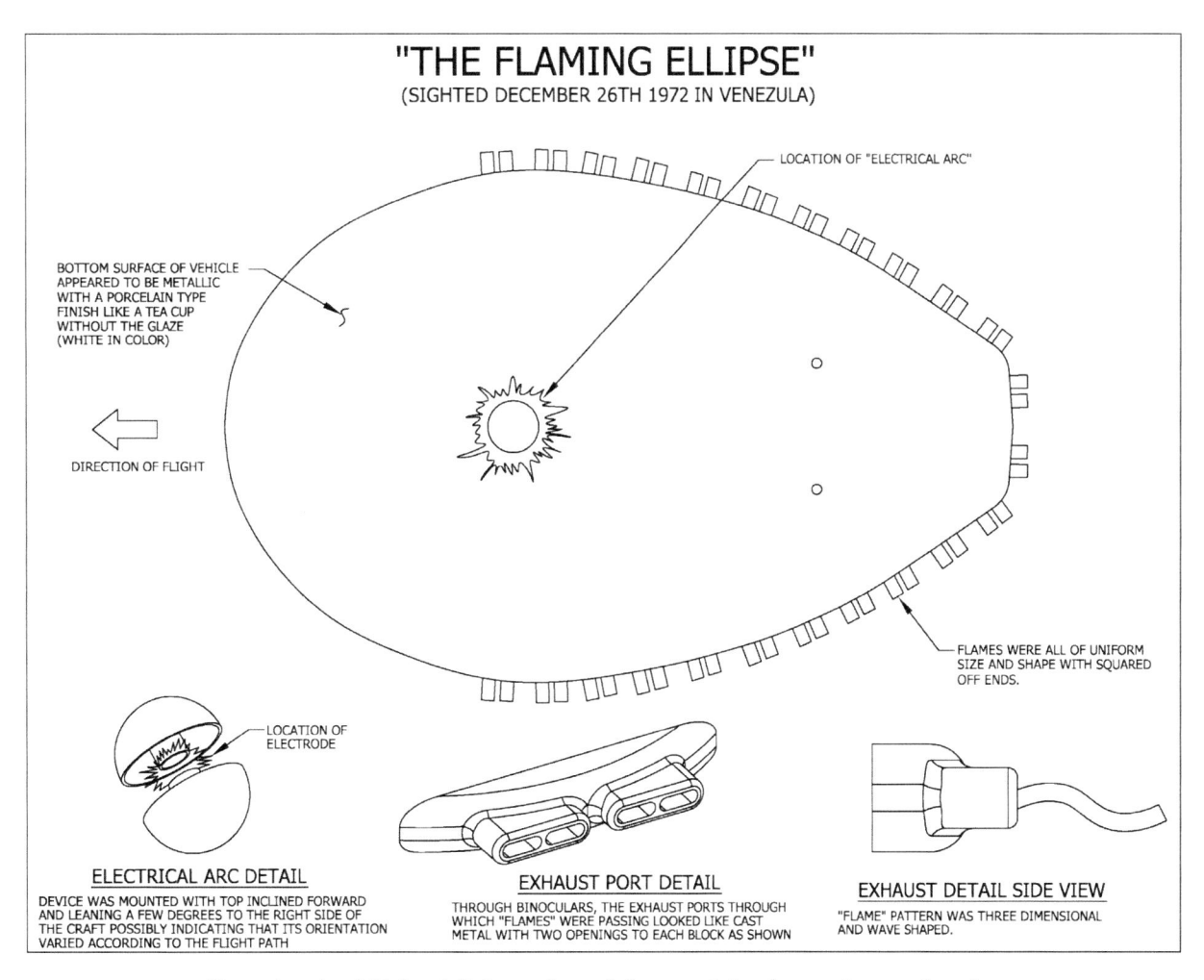

Drawing by Michael Schratt based from original eyewitness sketches

36" diameter opposed hemispherical type "insulators" and "electrodes" with spark gap as described by witness.

of binoculars from the neighbor. This second craft was identical in size, shape, and configuration to the first. The same "electrical" arc was seen in operation as observed on the first, which lit up its entire bottom surface. Around its perimeter, and starting about 1/3 of the way back on each side, were a series of "cast iron exhaust ports or vents." These vents were arranged in pairs, out of which exited uniquely shaped "flames" that resembled "lasagna noodles."

Through binoculars, these had the appearance not of actual fire exhaust, but of an electrical type discharge. Unique is the fact that all of the "flames" exited the ports in a similar three-dimensional wave design. Although there appeared to be movement within the "flames," their overall size and shape remained constant. As it neared the edge of the populated area of the city, this second vehicle accelerated, and passed by the airport flying the same pattern around the field as the first. Eventually, the craft continued on until it was lost in the distance. [Source: CUFOS archives, original report dated January 20, 1975.]

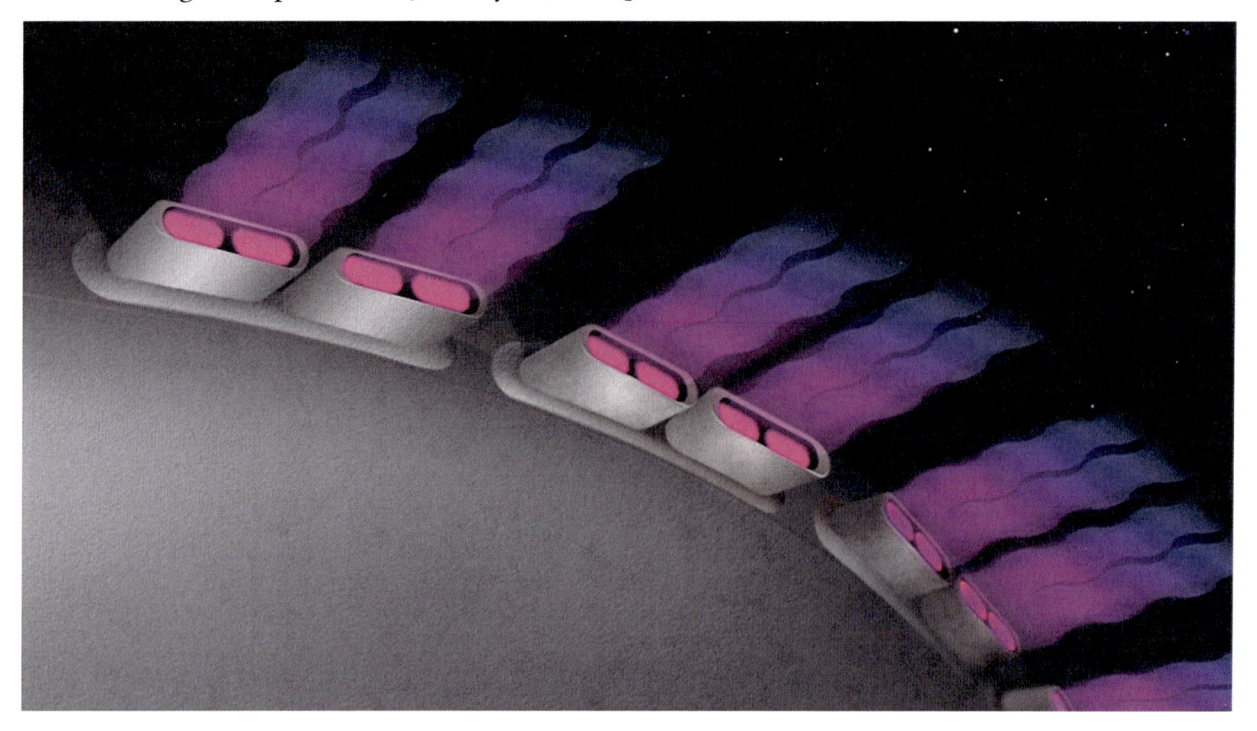

Electrical discharge "lasagna noodle" flames as described by the original eyewitness

U.S. ARMY RESERVE HELICOPTER UFO ENCOUNTER

October 18, 1973, Mansfield, OH

Of the many UFO reports by highly experienced pilots, few are as well documented as the case which occurred on the night of October 18, 1973 near Mansfield, Ohio. This significant CEII case involved a U.S. Army Reserve UH-1 helicopter, which had four crewmembers aboard. The sky was clear, visibility extended to 15 miles. During a return flight (around 10:55 p.m.) to Cleveland which originated from Columbus, Sgt. Robert J. Yanacsek alerted the other crewmembers that a red light was rapidly approaching from the east (Lt. A.D. Jezzi was flying at the time of the incident). Its closure rate on the helicopter was estimated to be approximately 700 mph. Thinking the unknown light may be from a military jet, Captain Lawrence J. Coyne grabbed the controls and performed an evasive maneuver by reducing power, and putting the helicopter into a steep dive. Then, the unknown object stopped and hovered above the helicopter. It was described by the crewmembers as looking like a cigar shaped craft (approximately 50 feet in length), with a dome on top. It had a gunmetal gray exterior appearance, with a steady red light on the front, and a white light on the back. The strange object made absolutely no noise.

Then a strange beam of green light could be seen originating from the bottom of the craft which illuminated the helicopter. Just minutes earlier, the helicopter was descending to an altitude of 1,700 feet. Now, as the strange craft departed to the west, the altimeter read 3,500 feet and CLIMBING at a rate of 1,000 feet per minute. Then, the crew felt a strange "bump", and leveled off at 3,800 feet which seemed to signify the end of the encounter. Attempts by the crew to establish radio contact with nearby Mansfield Airport failed for a period of ten minutes indicating the presents of an unusual electro-magnetic disturbance. Ground observers also witnessed the mid-air encounter making this case one of the most credible within the field of Ufology. Sources: NICAP, "Uninvited Guests" by Richard Hall

"SUNDAY NIGHT AT THE OSCARS"
MICHELIN MAN CASE #2
March 14, 1976, Liria, Spain

On March 14, 1976, Don Vicenta Corell (age 55) and his wife, Dona Carmen Civera (age 50), were returning home from their son's Naval Recruitment instruction ceremony in Liria, Spain. The time was 9:45 p.m. Once they left their son, they headed towards the main highway in the direction of Olocau. Their plan was to spend the night in the town of Museros. As they proceeded down the road, Dona observed a "very large light" just ahead, and to the left of their vehicle. The light was oval in shape, with rounded points. Soon thereafter, she saw a "spiral" coming out of the ground. Shockingly, the spiral transformed itself into a humanoid figure that resembled the "Michelin Man." The being was wearing a shiny dark colored suit that was tight around the legs, but puffed out around its upper body. Its arms were outstretched downward by its sides, and it had clenched fists. The strange being appeared to be floating approximately six inches off the ground. It moved with its feet together, and swayed from side to side. It was travelling in the same direction they were heading.

Before they caught up with it, the being stopped, and appeared to be looking at right angles to the road. As they passed it on the left side of the road, the electrical lighting system on their Renault-4 completely burned out causing their headlights to fail. In addition, the entire vehicle gave off a strange smoke, and an acrid burnt electrical odor. Driving in the dark now, Ms. Civera turned her head back and perceived that the humanoid was staring at them. They finally stopped approximately 650 feet beyond the being, and waved down two additional vehicles heading in the same direction. They asked both drivers if they had also seen the strange humanoid, which they replied that they had not. In a desperate attempt to describe what just occurred, Mr. Corell explained to the other drivers that he and his wife had both witnessed something that was "not of this world, but of another." Not wanting to be left stranded in their current situation without headlights, he drove his vehicle between the other two that they had stopped, and made their way to the town of Betera. After that, they left their car, and proceeded safely to their final destination of Museros in one of the other two vehicles. [Source: Gray Barker UFO Collection (Clarksburg WV).]

"GLASS BUBBLE" UFO WITH OCCUPANTS
June 22, 1976, Canary Islands

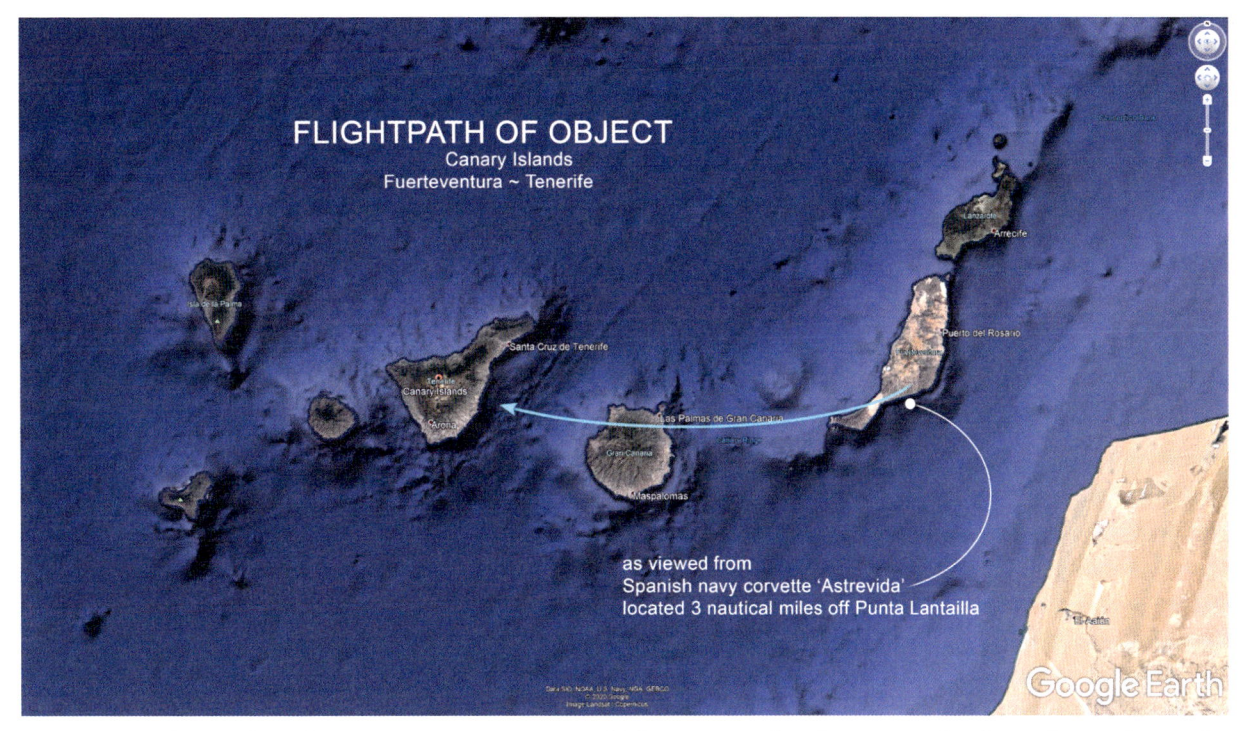

FLIGHTPATH OF OBJECT
Canary Islands
Fuerteventura ~ Tenerife

as viewed from
Spanish navy corvette 'Astrevida'
located 3 nautical miles off Punta Lantailla

On the night of June 22, 1976, an incredible series of sightings took place throughout the Spanish Canary Islands from east to west. At 9:27 p.m., the corvette *Atrevida*, of the Spanish Navy, was positioned three nautical miles from Punta Lantilla, off the southern coast of Fuerteventura. The ship's Commanding Officer, and multiple personnel on-board the ship, witnessed a vivid yellow/blue-colored light that was moving from the shore towards their position. It was climbing, and once it attained a certain altitude, it remained stationary. Then, a great halo of yellowish/bluish light developed, and remained in the same position for approximately 40 minutes. Two minutes later, the light split into two parts, the smaller part being beneath, inside the luminous halo. The upper part began to climb in a spiraling motion, and finally vanished.

The next series of sightings took place over the northern tip of Grand Canary Island in a town called Las Rosas. Dr. Padron Leon was visiting a patient at the time of the encounter. The patient's son was with him, and both were in a taxi, on their way to care for his sick mother. Suddenly, they reported seeing a gigantic ball of "electric blue color," hovering approximately 6 feet above the ground. It was about 150 feet away. The doctor stressed that the sphere was so perfectly configured that it looked like it was "laid out with a compass." Next, they both had the sensation of extreme cold, and the taxicab driver began trembling. All three noticed that the taxi's radio had mysteriously cut out. The strange "glass bubble" remained stationary, and they could see two giant "figures" inside. Their sighting lasted approximately 20 minutes at very close range, which allowed them to provide some very specific details.

Detail view of the luminous light as observed by the crew of the Spanish Naval warship Atrevida

The "glass bubble" was transparent, and they could see the stars in the sky behind it. It was about 20 feet in diameter, and had a silver-colored "platform" near its lower surface. On top of the platform, they could see three round "consoles" or "panels." The beings were 9 feet tall, and were wearing one-piece tight-fitting flight suits. They also wore what looked like black "diver's helmets," over their disproportionately large heads. Their hands appeared to be enclosed in some type of sheath or cone shaped device. They were facing each other, and appeared to be operating some type of levers or "controls." The driver switched on his big spotlight, and when he did, the object rose vertically until it was even with the top of a nearby house. Then, they saw a transparent tube inside the sphere that rose up vertically from the base of the platform. Blue-colored smoke was rising out of the sphere and filled the inside. Next, the bubble grew in size until it was as large as a 20-story building. The two beings however, remained their original height.

All three eyewitnesses were terrified at the sight, and the driver quickly turned around and headed for some nearby houses. Once inside, the homeowner indicated that their television set had just blacked out. They remained inside with the family, and could see the giant sphere from the window. As it expanded to an incredible size, the blue gas inside stopped moving. Then, in a flash, after giving out a *high-pitched whistle*, the object shot away towards the Island of Tenerife. As it departed, it changed configuration into a spindle-shaped object, surrounded by a large, white halo. [Sources: "Unidentified Flying Objects Briefing Document, The Best Available Evidence" by Don Berliner and Antonio Huneeus December 1995, *Flying Saucer Review*, Vol. 23, No. 3, 1977, *Adjutant's Report*, Las Palmas Aerial Sector, July 16, 1976]

Luminous phenomenon as observed by residents of Las Rosas (Grand Canary Island)

Detail view of "Glass Bubble UFO" with occupants seen by multiple eyewitnesses in Las Rosas

"FAT FRISBEE" SIGHTING #2
December 1976, Dana Point, CA

During December of 1976, a Dana Point, California mother and her two children (daughter age 16, son 3) were driving westbound on Blue Lantern Street near Pacific Coast Highway. The time was 7:30 p.m., when suddenly, they saw a huge bright rotating object approach, and hover in front of their car at very close range. The UFO was described as looking like a "fat Frisbee," and had a blinking red light on top, with thousands of multi-colored, randomly flashing computer processing lights located around its outer circumference. The strange object appeared to fill up half the windshield as viewed from inside their automobile, a 1976 Pontiac Grand Prix. The primary eyewitness rolled down her window, but heard no noise coming from the craft. All three watched in fascination for approximately three to five minutes before the UFO made two 90 degree turns before it sped away westbound toward the ocean. [Source: CUFOS archives.]

FAT FRISBEE UFO
(SIGHTED DECEMBER 1976 IN DANA POINT CALIFORNIA)
CRAFT HAD THOUSANDS OF COMPUTER LIKE LIGHTS
ALONG ITS UPPER AND LOWER CIRCUMFERENCE

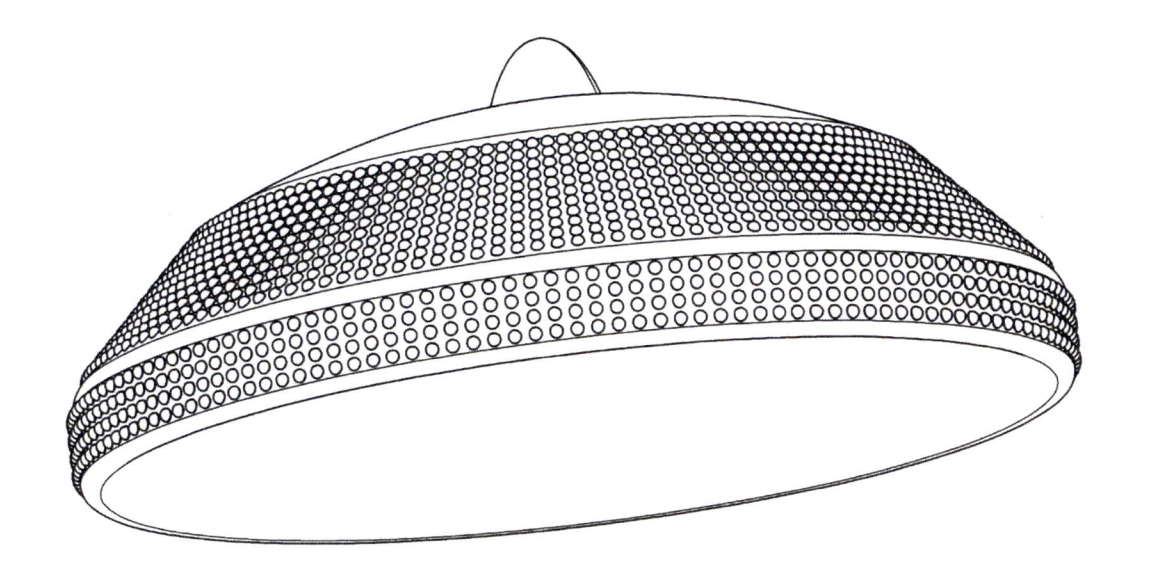

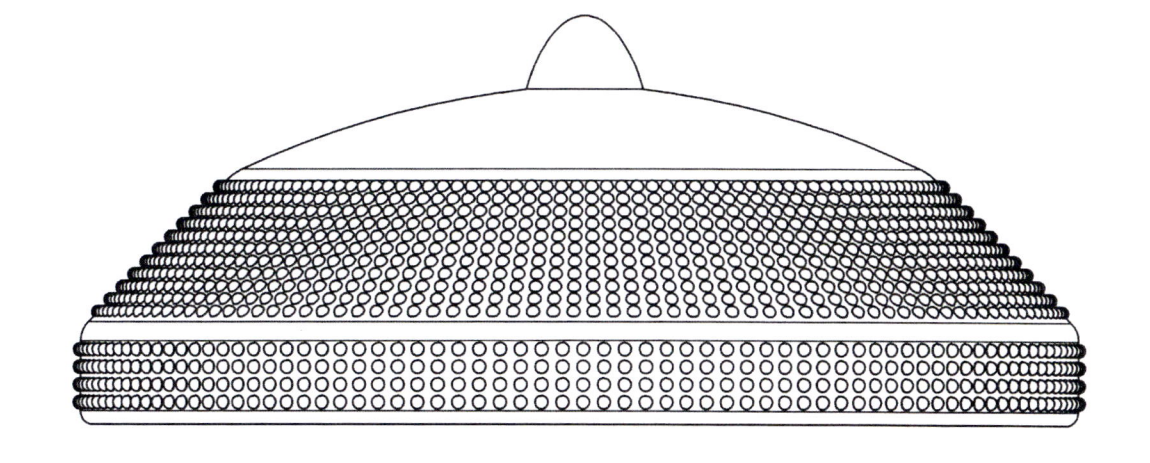

CLASSIFIED

80

THE "ORANGE JUICER" WITH TENTACLES
September 10, 1976, Colusa, CA

Bill Pecha (age 39) was watching television in his home around 12:45 a.m. on September 10, 1976. He was living in Colusa, California at the time of the incident. His wife and two children (aged 8 and 10) were sleeping. Suddenly, and without warning, the TV and air-conditioning unit went dead. Thinking a circuit might have blown, he walked outside to check the circuit breaker box. As he approached the corner of his mobile home, he could feel the sensation of an electrostatic charge in the immediate area. He was shocked to see the hair on his chest, arms and head begin to stand up. In addition, his hair began to crackle and snap, similar to the effect when running a nylon comb through dry hair rapidly. At that exact instant, he looked up and saw a large, 140-foot diameter disc-shaped craft hovering silently 50 feet above the ground. He could see it in great detail due to the full moon. The strange craft had no rivets, seams, bolts or screws visible on its exterior surface.

It had a vertically ribbed dome on top that resembled a "lemon juice squeezer." The dome's texture, and its immediate flared out base had the appearance of mildly rough and porous "slag." This upper area was dark gray in color. The second rounded and flared out area leading toward the edge of the craft looked similar to porcelain. The edges of the craft, and the perimeter that was rotating clockwise, looked like stainless steel. A smaller section on the bottom of the disc contained a powerful spotlight that was shining down on the ground. This area was rotating counter-clockwise at a slower rate than the outer edge. Clearly visible, were six dangling "conduit pipes" with frayed ends, which hung down 6 to 8 feet from the bottom of the disc. Then, the craft slowly retreated to the back of his property. At that moment, these appendages (conduit pipes) retracted inside the UFO. Two hook-like devices also retracted upwards, but remained partially visible. Simultaneously, two "hatches" opened up on either side of the disc from which appeared a "goose-neck" lighting apparatus.

These were directed downward, and emitted a bluish/white beam of light. Mr. Pecha could see that they were made out of some type flexible tubing. By now, the craft was maneuvering over a nearby neighbor's house, and he could see that the surrounding area was lit up like daylight. At that moment, he noticed two smaller craft that were hovering over the 500,000-volt power lines nearby. These two identical craft appeared to be almost resting on the lines, each one between two towers, but separated by one span section. Each UFO was shining a powerful column of white light from its side edges down onto the power lines. The lines themselves were glowing red for some distance out on each side. Visibly shaken, he ran into the house and woke up his wife. Proceeding to the back of their home, he pulled back the curtains and could see the large craft through the window. It was hovering next to a nearby airfield, and lit up everything like daylight. His wife, Lenda Pecha, also saw the strange scene that was unfolding through the bedroom window. Suddenly, the large craft sped off at an incredible speed towards the foothills, which were approximately 20 miles to the west. According to Mr. Pecha, the UFO covered this distance in about 2-3 seconds, and he could see that it illuminated the hills with its spotlight. Incredibly, the strange craft *flew back* to its original position in just a few seconds, *all without causing a sonic boom.*

Now, in fear for the safety of his family, Pecha decided to quickly gather his family to vacate the premises. Just then, he noticed the two smaller UFOs break away, and shoot up out of sight. Frantically, he pulled on an old pair of jeans, grabbed the children with his wife, and headed for the door. Just then, the TV and air conditioner came back on. Piling the family inside his new pickup truck, he backed out of the driveway to escape. As he raced down the blacktop road towards town at 90 mph, he noticed that the larger UFO was now following them. He was frantically trying to put some distance between his truck and the UFO despite driving with the headlights turned off to avoid attracting any attention to his vehicle. As they drove along, he could see the large craft pull up to one side of his vehicle, and then cross over to the other side. Reaching his close friend's house at the edge of town, Pecha skidded to a stop in their front yard. At that point, he leaped out and began banging on the front door. By this time, the craft had moved out over town, and was somewhat higher in the sky. Les Arant and his wife Gayle answered the door to see a shaken and disheveled Bill Pecha standing in front of them. All four adults (including two children) then observed the craft angle up in a gradual climb, and disappear in the direction of Sacramento. [Sources: CUFOS archives, *Sun Herald* May 29, 1979. *The UFO Evidence* Vol. 2, by Richard Hall 2001.]

Trying to escape the UFO, Bill Pecha drives his pickup truck down a moonlit road at 90 mph.

Six eyewitnesses observe the large UFO just before it accelerates and ascends out of sight

A BELL IN THE BACKYARD

November 6, 1976, Virginia Beach, VA

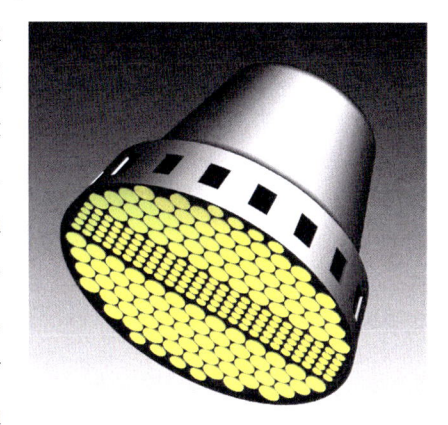

On November 6, 1976 Mrs. Barbara Nielson of Virginia Beach, Virginia, spotted a bell-shaped UFO which hovered approximately 2 feet off the ground in her back yard. The craft had a light on top that blinked on and off from red to white. It had rectangular shaped windows near the bottom which emitted a phosphorescent light. The object rotated in a counter-clockwise direction, while it tipped up along its vertical axis. The UFO measured 5 feet high, and 5 feet wide. The primary eyewitnesses noticed a faint humming sound emanating from the craft. The bottom of the object was comprised of multiple yellow-colored lights. Mrs. Nielson got the impression that the craft was under remote control due to the fact that it swung back and forth "like a bell." There were black symbols running across the center section (similar to the "newsflash" scrolling text seen in Times Square). Shortly thereafter, the object sped off across the nearby highway. [Source: Wendelle Stevens Collection.]

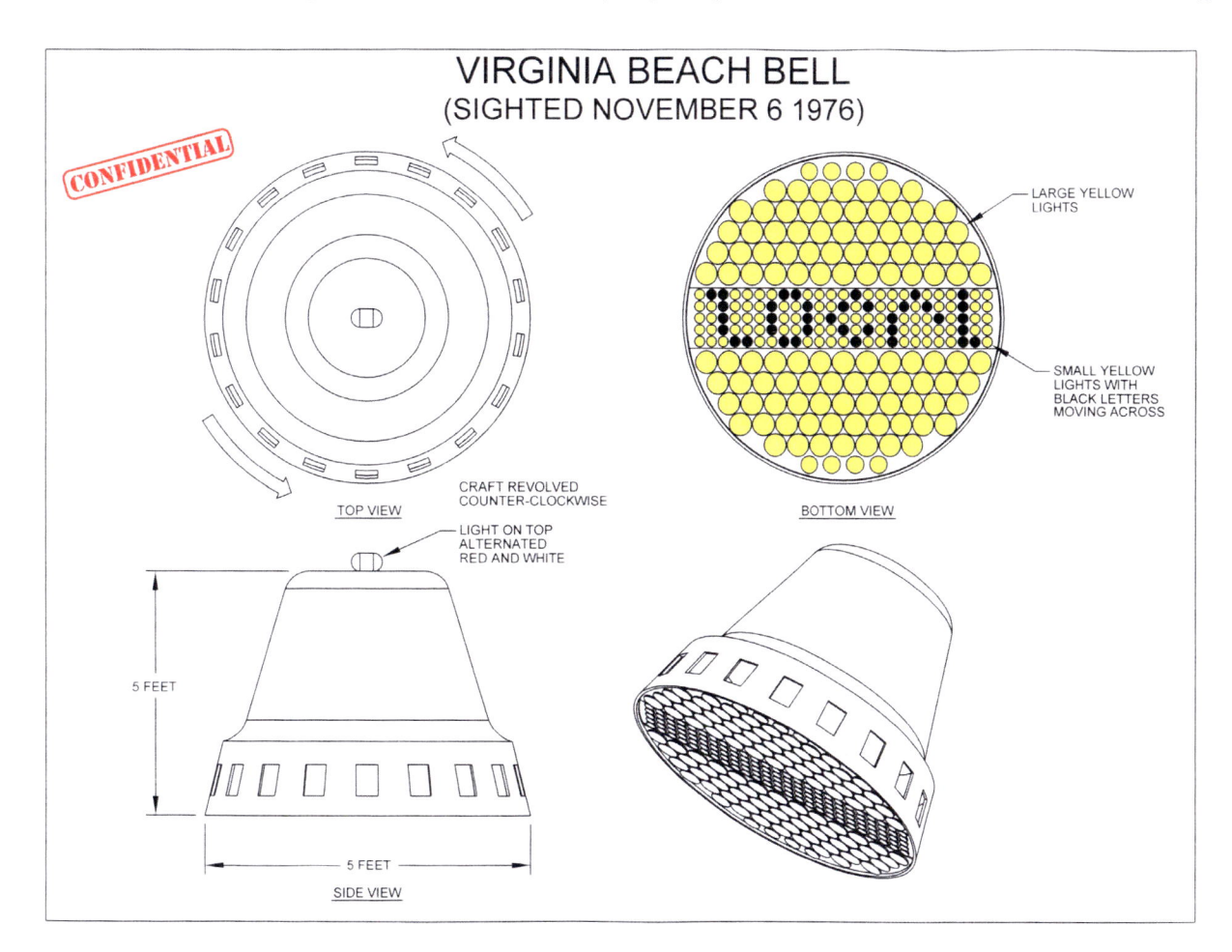

SIGHTING OF INFLATABLE BEING IN CAPSULE

February 10, 1977, Tucson, AZ

Drawing by Rudy Gardea

A new and spectacular kind of close encounter UFO case took place on February 10, 1977 in Tucson, Arizona. It was 7:30 p.m. when Ms. Lois Stovall was sitting in the middle of the couch on the south side of her living room. From this perspective, she could easily see Lillian Cavett Elementary School through her front window. Suddenly, she noticed a bright light or flame rising just to the left of the school. Her attention was captured by the strange beauty of the light which seemed to rise and come around the southwest corner of the school. It then curved toward her house, and descended to within a few inches of the ground, almost directly in front of her house, but still on the school side of the street. It hovered in that position momentarily, and then began to move again. Lois told her grandmother, also sitting in the living room, and the both got up and went to the door for a better view.

They both saw it begin to rise and move south towards the school fence and their house. It came over the fence and into their yard where it hovered for a few minutes. Stovall and her grandmother went out into the yard and stood less than 50 feet from the object and watched in amazement. The object was cylindrical/capsule shaped and featured blunt rounded ends on both the top and bottom. It measured approximately 3 feet in diameter, and 6 feet high. The top was slightly more rounded than the bottom, and the object seemed to be facing them directly. The cylindrical side, between the top and bottom ends featured a transparent "cut-out" window section. They could now see the source of the bright light which first caught their attention. The light resembled a beautiful multi-colored flame, with streams of red and blue fire which originated from the bottom of the capsule. The front part of the craft featured a clear transparent "windshield" section with dark colored "bars" that ran from top to bottom. These bars appeared to be positioned in front of the windshield.

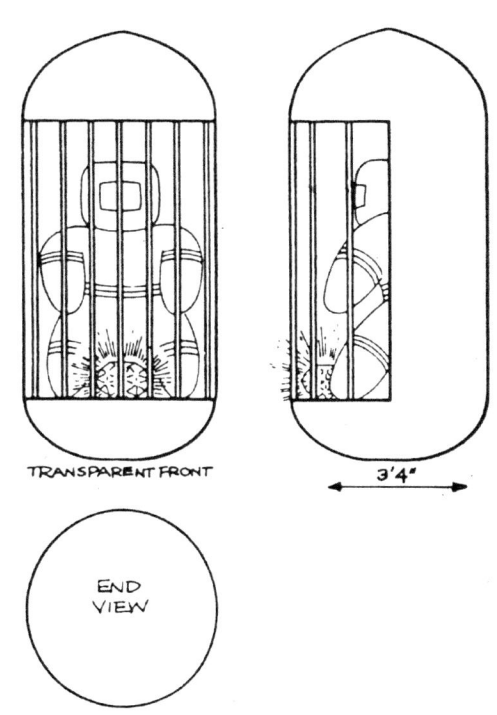

Original APRO report drawing

Behind the bars crouched a human-shaped figure which was completely gray in color. It appeared to be wearing what looked like an inflatable bio-hazard suit. It featured ridges or rings near the ends of its appendages. No distinct facial features were observed, and no hands or feet could be seen. The figure was standing in the small, close-fitting cabin in a crouched position with its hands slightly forward and positioned above its knees. It appeared to be about the size of a 6-year-old child. Mrs. Alice Buckner, the grandmother of Lois and owner of the house, stood directly under the craft and was able to reach up with her right hand to within 2 feet of the

Drawing of being with bars removed for clarity by Rudy Gardea

bottom of the object. She wanted to touch it to see what it was, but it was slightly beyond her reach. As she did so, it began to rise at an angle heading toward the south.

Lois said she heard a "click" just before it started to move up, but Buckner, who was directly under the front of the craft, said that she didn't hear anything. As she reached up, Buckner said, "there's a man in there!" She could see the small puffy figure crouched behind the "flame," and she could determine that it was a suit, seemingly inflated like a balloon. There was a rectangular window on the front section where the head/face would be. Alice thought that she could barely make out a face, but was unable to distinguish any specific features. Then, the craft began to rise, and all she could see was the bottom. She was unable to see any features of the interior cabin such as a seat, controls, lights, dials or instrument panel. She did see that the unusual multi-colored light was on the floor near the little figure's feet.

One interesting aspect of this bizarre encounter is the repeated references by the witnesses to multiple helicopters which were located directly over the schoolyard at the time of the sighting. Initially, there were three helicopters with glowing red cabin lights flying at very low altitudes over the school grounds while the small capsule was being observed. One of the m passed directly over the craft at less than treetop level and then flew towards the west. The others crisscrossed the school grounds while the ship was hovering. Then, when it was climbing away to the south, as Lois followed it around the house, she saw 5 or 6 helicopters in that direction. Investigators who contacted the local area Air Traffic Control Center were told they had no record of any Army helicopter flights through Tucson airspace on the evening of the incident. [Source: *APRO Bulletin* February 1977.]

UFO ENCOUNTER WITH CEII EFFECTS
January 1978, Fort Smith, AR

During January of 1978, residents of Arkansas had an astonishing series of UFO encounters. The first report came from a Fort Smith law enforcement official. He described seeing several people who were looking up in the sky at a series of strange lights. Inquiries to the Federal Aviation Administration came back negative. The second sighting originated from two newspaper reporters (also from Fort Smith) who described seeing a strange craft that was about half the size of a Volkswagen, and gray metallic in color. The object emitted an unusual beeping noise. Electromagnetic effects included stalled engines, electrical system malfunctions, and radios that went dead. When the craft departed, all electrical systems within the vicinity returned to normal. The third sighting involved a mother and her two children. While driving home to Alma, Arkansas around 10:00 p.m., all three spotted a dazzling array of multi-colored lights coming over the top of the trees. The lights stayed motionless for a few moments, and then disappeared back over the trees. [Source: *Argus Press* Feb 2, 1978]

FARM LANDING SURPRISE
May 1978, Weeley, England

In May of 1978, Peter Duncan of Weeley, England, had an interesting nighttime encounter with a UFO. He described seeing a brilliant flash of light out on his farm, which he originally thought was a helicopter. Upon further inspection, he quickly determined that his initial assessment was incorrect. Mr. Duncan claims that he was no more than 20 yards from a strange looking craft that had landed on his property. The UFO was described as having a mushroom shaped dome on top, with a middle section that appeared to have a series of slit-shaped port holes. He also reported seeing a ramp extended out of the craft.

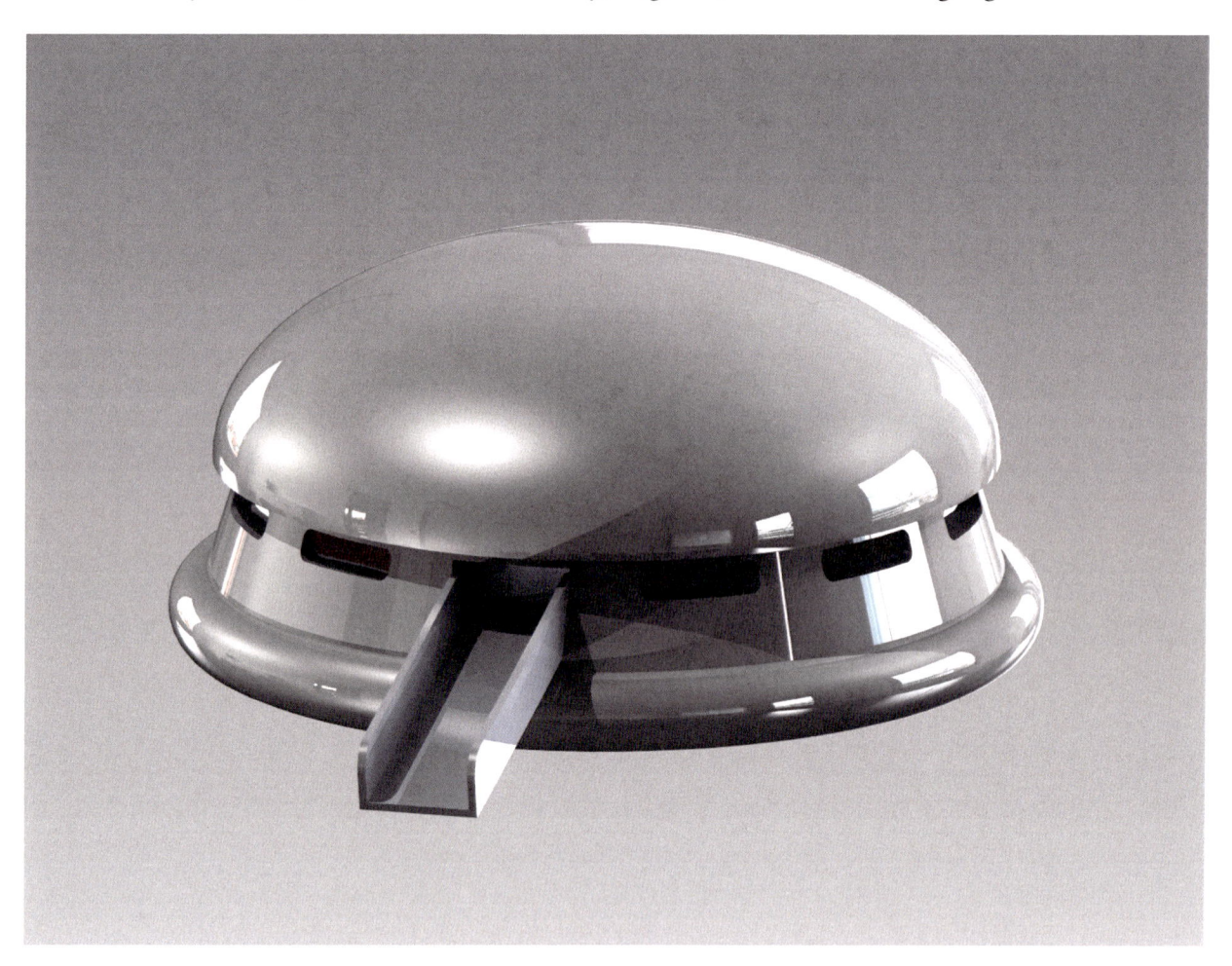

The bottom measured approximately 90 feet across, and it was making a constant buzzing noise. Mr. Duncan stated that he was originally terrified, but slowly moved closer to the craft to get a better look. Then, the object lifted up, and sped out of sight. Out of fear of ridicule, he reported his sighting eight months after the event took place. [Source: *East Essex Gazette* January 12, 1979.]

SAUCER WITH PIPE ENCOUNTER
September 11, 1980, Anderson, SC

Illustration by John MacNeill

In the early morning hours of September 11, 1980 Mr. Jerry McAllister, a resident of Anderson, South Carolina was awakened by a brilliant light. He quickly jumped out of bed and witnessed a large luminous object hovering in a horizontal position. Mr. McAllister also alerted his wife, and urged her to view the object as well. The craft was no more than 150 feet away, and approximately 40 feet above the tree-tops. The object was completely surrounded with multiple halogen-like headlights which lit up the surrounding area like day, and it emitted an ear shattering noise. Above the lights were a row of rectangular shaped windows which emanated a deep purple colored light, and measured 6-feet x 8-feet.

There was a smooth raised "seam" located immediately above the windows, which ran along the entire circumference of the object. The bottom surface of the craft was flat and dark in color. A small red light could be seen which was connected to a curved pipe-like structure that was located on the bottom of the craft. Mr. McAllister contacted the Anderson County Sheriff's office, and Deputy Mike Burton arrived at the scene in time to witness the UFOs departure. Residual effects on the witnesses from the craft included the following: eye irritation, ringing in

ANDERSON SOUTH CAROLINA
(SEPTEMBER 11, 1980)

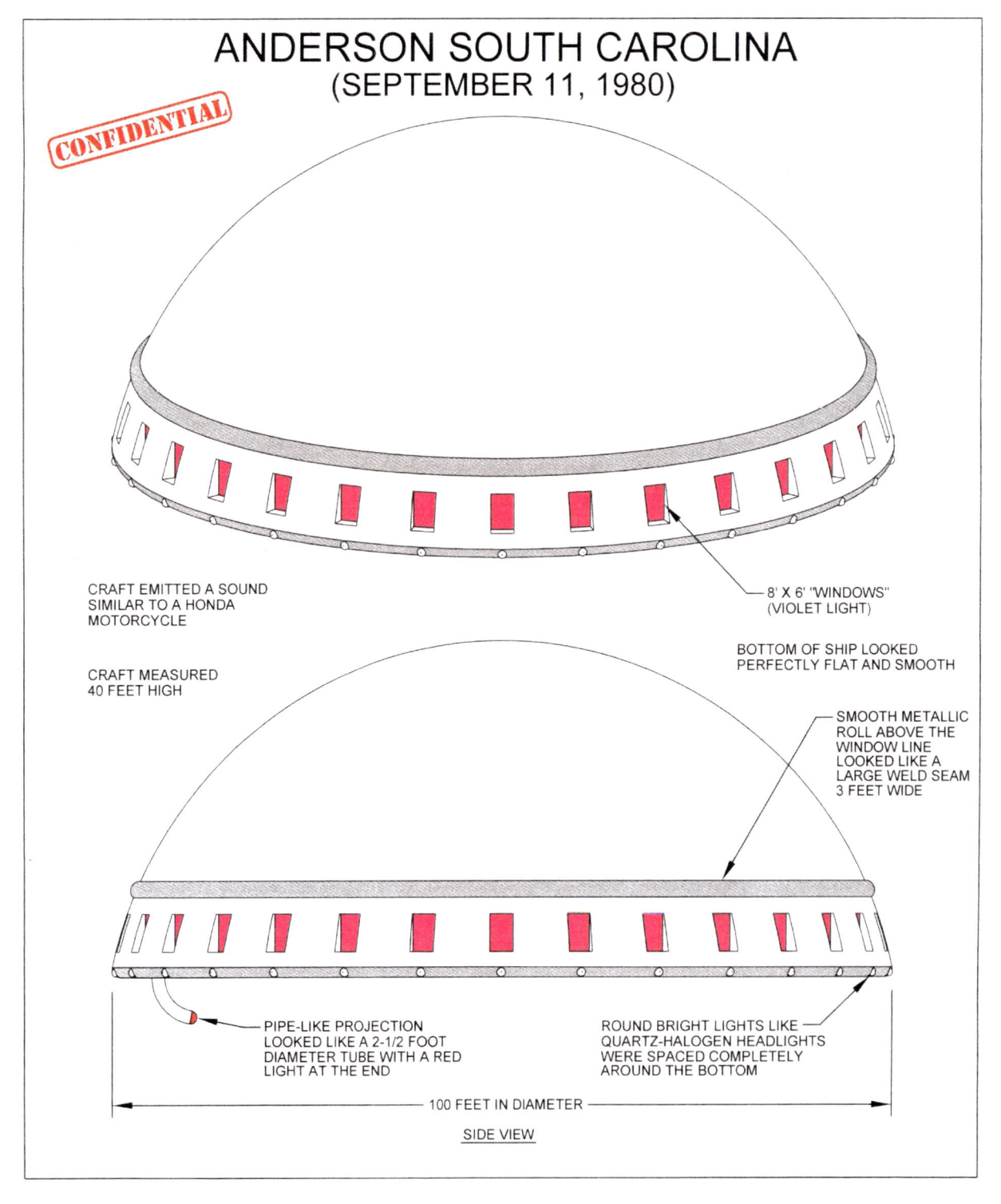

CONFIDENTIAL

- CRAFT EMITTED A SOUND SIMILAR TO A HONDA MOTORCYCLE
- CRAFT MEASURED 40 FEET HIGH
- 8' X 6' "WINDOWS" (VIOLET LIGHT)
- BOTTOM OF SHIP LOOKED PERFECTLY FLAT AND SMOOTH
- SMOOTH METALLIC ROLL ABOVE THE WINDOW LINE LOOKED LIKE A LARGE WELD SEAM 3 FEET WIDE
- PIPE-LIKE PROJECTION LOOKED LIKE A 2-1/2 FOOT DIAMETER TUBE WITH A RED LIGHT AT THE END
- ROUND BRIGHT LIGHTS LIKE QUARTZ-HALOGEN HEADLIGHTS WERE SPACED COMPLETELY AROUND THE BOTTOM
- 100 FEET IN DIAMETER

SIDE VIEW

the ears and headaches. Evidence of dangerous radiation was found in the nearby soil where the craft had hovered, and also on pine needles. A recommendation was made that the area under the ship's hovering position be roped off. [Source: Wendelle Stevens collection (confirmed by NICAP), *Easley Progress* September 17, 1980.]

STRANGE ENCOUNTER WITH OCCUPANTS OVER ALABAMA

February 3, 1983, Mobile, AL

Illustration by John MacNeill

It was the evening of February 3, 1983, when Pat Norris was returning home from a visit to her friend's house in Mobile, Alabama. She was heading home on Highway 90, when she exited the expressway, and heard a loud explosion. The car began vibrating violently, so she pulled off to the side of the road. Thinking the transmission might have fallen out, she opened the car door and leaned over to look under the vehicle. Everything appeared to be in working order, so she continued her trip home. It was at this point that she noticed that the wooded area in front of her was brilliantly lit. She initially thought that some type of helicopter search was taking place due to the lights. It was at this point, that she stopped the car again and noticed a huge object about a half-mile west of her location.

The strange craft was gigantic, and measured approximately 210 feet long, and 80 feet high. It appeared to be moving towards her at about 5 mph. She also recalled hearing a "chopping wind noise, a high-pitched sound, and a roaring sound." She also noted hearing something that sounded like the "whipping of the wind, or a tornado." When the object reached a point fairly close to her location it stopped, and the noise ceased. Everything now was completely quiet. At this point, Mrs. Norris got out of her car to get a better look at the strange object. She estimated that the

Illustration by John MacNeill

total duration of her sighting to be about five minutes. The craft had a "top deck" of elongated windows that she estimated to be about 50 feet across. Within these windows, she could see approximately 20 to 30 beings walking around. They were apparently oblivious to her presence. The wall behind them was curved, and everything appeared to have an antiseptically sterile atmosphere.

The beings had pale skin, and were dressed in one-piece tight-fitting suits. She judged them to be about 5-feet, 10-inches tall, and of slender build. The top of their heads appeared to be more prominent, and they had no hair. Below this top deck, there was an opaque window which was divided into sections and inset into the craft. Near the bottom of the craft, there was a door which was closing from right to left. Mrs. Norris got a brief view inside this section of the craft, and noticed a "black asphalt" road inside. On the left side, there appeared to be a wall which was composed of multiple "tubes, pipes and cylinders." Running across the entire craft, she could see what looked like "rivets" and "portholes." As she peered into these portholes, she recalled seeing "huge I-beams," bulkheads and stringers, which reminded her of a vast "dry dock" where ships are constructed. The bottom side of the craft was tiered upwards as it progressed towards the back.

On the underside of the craft, she could see what looked like highly-polished, reflective mirrors that measured 12-inches X 12-inches across. Together, these mirrors made up the formation of a large cross. Two observation decks or "gondolas" protruded from the bottom of the craft which included the same 5 feet, 10-inches tall beings from the upper portion. She could hear a very low-pitched "growling" noise emanating from this area. She also noticed four "pipes" protruding from the front of the craft about six or eight feet. They were set in three-foot square "boxes," and reminded her of a "weapon." As it moved away, the strange craft lit up the wooded area near her. She could see white spotlights, and to the side, blue and red lights that intermingled, pointing to the clouds and then down to earth. The craft eventually took a southerly turn and disappeared from her location. [Source: *APRO Bulletin* Vol. 32 No. 2 1984.]

"MOTHERSHIP" SIGHTED BY AIRLINE CAPTAIN

November 17, 1986, Eastern, AK

It was 6:13 p.m. on the night of November 17, 1986, when Japan Airlines Flight 1628 was near the end of the Iceland-to-Anchorage leg of its flight from Paris to Tokyo. The cargo 747 was flying at an altitude of 39,000 feet over Ft. Yukon, Alaska, at an airspeed of 0.84 Mach or 525 knots. Its crew included Captain Kenju Terauchi (age 47), First Officer Takanori Tamefuji, and Flight Engineer Yoshio Tsukuda. Suddenly, Captain Terauchi noticed two strange craft from his cockpit window about 30 degrees to his left or port side. They were at a distance of approximately seven to 8 nautical miles away. The Captain confirmed the distance by using his on-board Bendix color radar. Initially, he thought they might be military aircraft, so he called Anchorage Flight Control to see if there was any traffic in his vicinity. Anchorage replied "the only traffic is you." They appeared to be cylindrical in shape, and about the size of a DC-8 jet or 150 feet across. Looking straight on, they resembled two "cube"-shaped objects, and all three crew members could see them. The Captain dimmed the lights just to confirm he wasn't seeing any reflections.

Down the center of each craft, they could see what looked like a dark-colored band which separated multiple levels of amber colored lights. These lights appeared to be rotating in opposite directions. Suddenly, the craft came within 500 to 1,000 feet of the plane. At this point, all three crew members could feel "heat on their faces" from the strange UFOs. The objects were rapidly changing direction, and stayed with the 747 (on its port side) for approximately 35 minutes, despite it taking evasive maneuvers, and descending to an altitude of 31,000 feet. However, the two unknown craft descended with him "in formation." South of Fairbanks, Terauchi executed a full 360 degree turn in an effort to "shake off" the strange objects, but they continued their close proximity flying parallel to his aircraft. Eventually, the two UFOs departed the area, and Captain Terauchi lost visual contact with the craft 40 nautical miles north of Talkeetna..

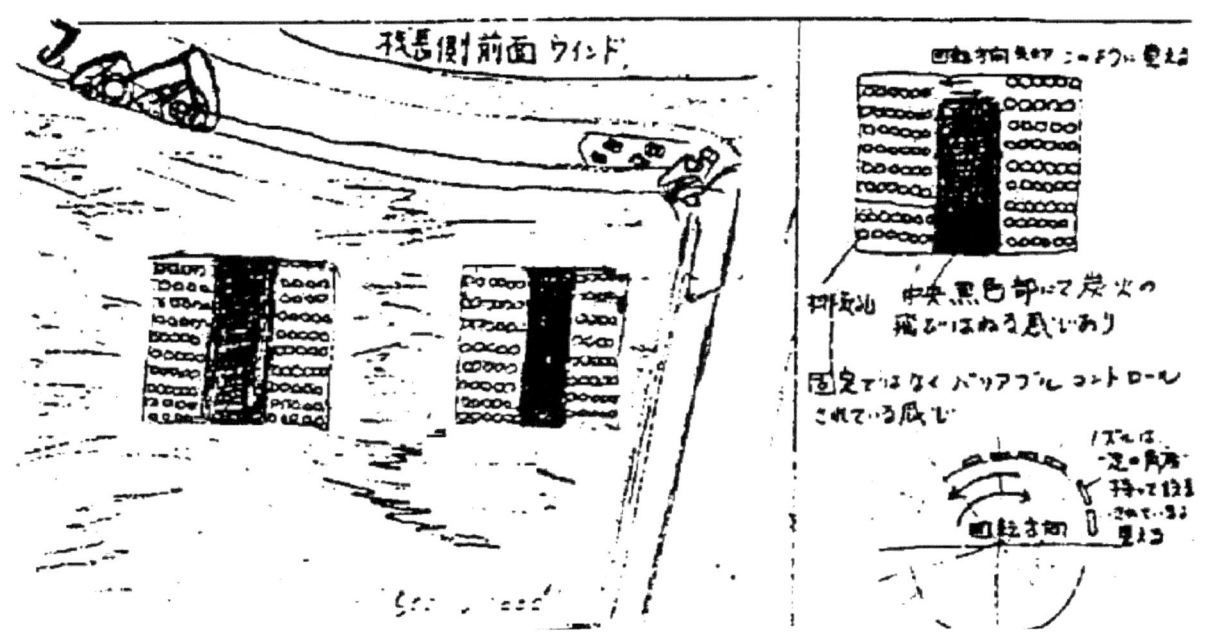

Original sketch by Captain Terauchi depicting what the two initial UFOs looked like from the cockpit window.

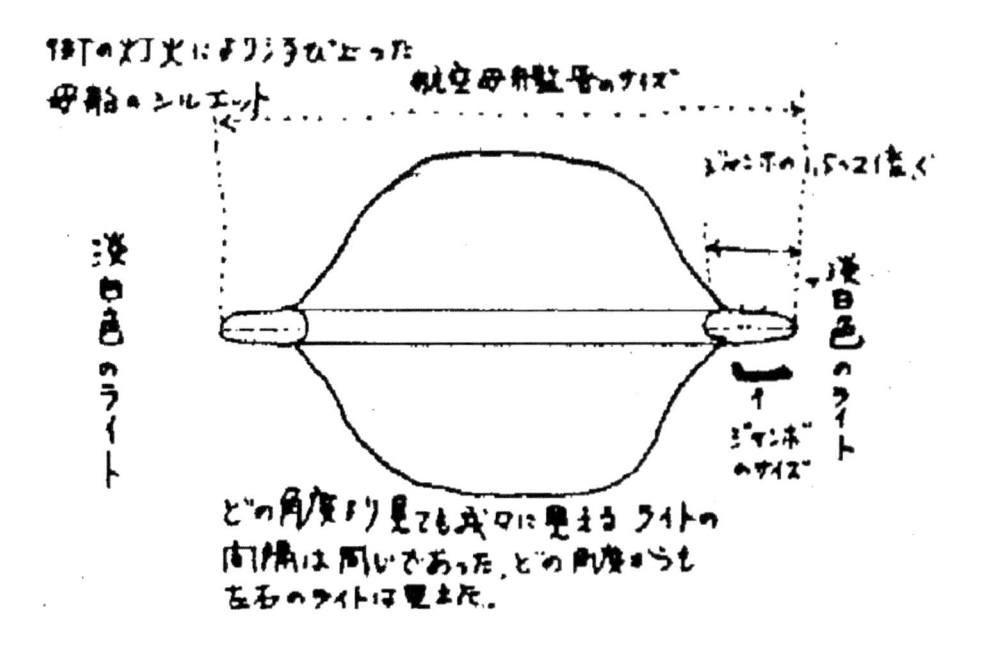

Original sketch by Captain Terauchi depicting large "Mothership" on the night of November 17, 1986

After the initial sighting of the two UFOs, a much larger "Mothership" approached from behind the aircraft and "shadowed" it for more than 300 miles. Captain Terauchi stated he could see the silhouette of the object since it was being back-lit from the city lights below. The massive craft was spherical or "walnut" in shape, and had a large, wrap-around flange protruding from its exterior. As incredible as it may sound, Captain Terauchi described the UFO as being "twice the size of an aircraft carrier." He also stated that it "dwarfed our 747." Eventually, the unknown craft departed, and Flight 1628 landed without further incident. Ground based Federal Aviation Administration (FAA) air traffic controllers tracked the object on their long-range radar for more than 32 minutes. In addition, military Air Force radar as well as the 747s on-board weather radar confirmed the sighting.

Upon landing in Anchorage, the flight crew was interviewed by FAA officials, and found to be "normal, rational and professional" people, with no drug or alcohol problems. [Sources: "Unidentified Flying Objects Briefing Document, The Best Available Evidence," By Don Berliner and Antonio Huneeus, December 1995, *New York Times* January 6, 1987, *Newsweek* January 12, 1987, *New York City Tribune* January 29, 1987, *Daily News* (Associated Press) January 6, 1987, *The Miami Herald* December 30, 1986, *Miami Herald* January 4, 1987, *Mainichi Daily News* January 14, 1987.]

Captain Terauchi describes his incredible encounter with a UFO to the press

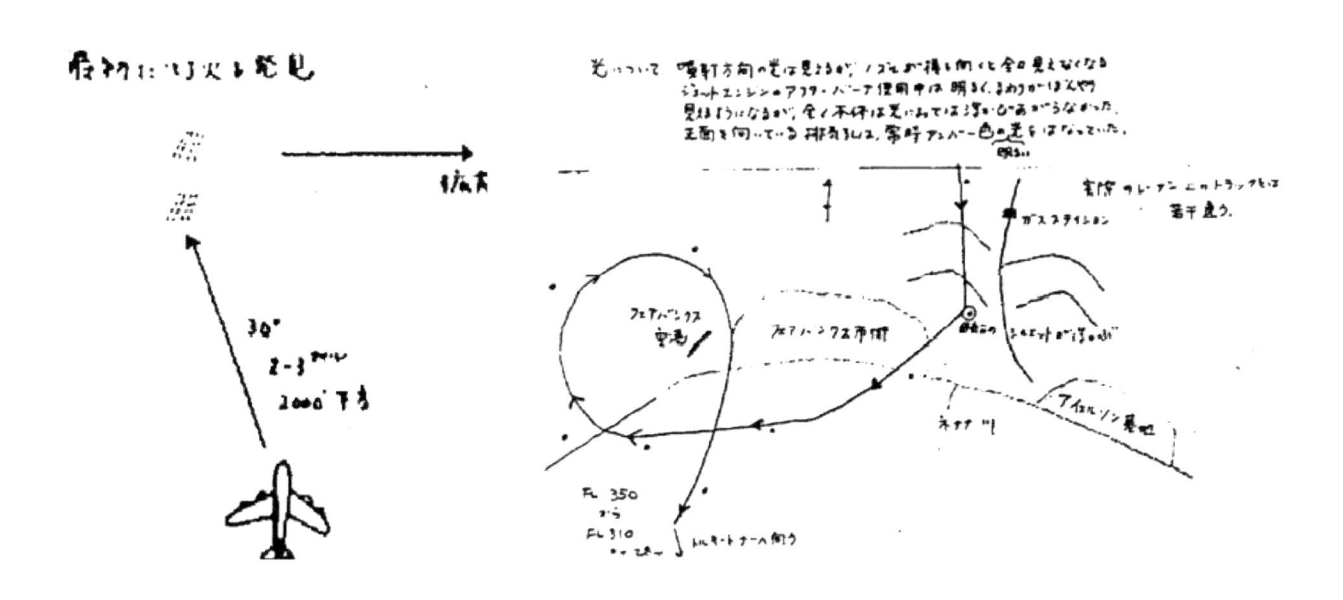

*Sketch shows UFOs
8 miles from plane*

*Terauchi's 747 flight path sketch
highlighting 360-degree turn*

CONNING TOWER UFO
May 14, 1988, Gresham, OR

Letter received by CUFOS from Valerie C. (last name on file) dated March 11, 1997. It has been reproduced here for historical purposes. The following is a paraphrased account from a six- page report of a UFO sighting Gresham, Oregon, May 14, 1988.

The time of the sighting was 9:45 p.m. The circumstances were as follows. My friend, Tom S. (last name on file), and I had dined out in Vancouver, Washington, driven back along the Columbia River and crossed over into Oregon on I-205. It was a clear moonless night. The music from the car radio was soothing, and I had laid my head back on the seat and closed my eyes. Tom exited from I-205, and swung the car onto 84N, going east toward Gresham. Six or seven minutes later we topped the rise on the freeway at 181st, and as we began the assent on the other side, Tom spotted wavering lights rotating to the left of and about 60 feet above the freeway. I heard him gasp, "what in the hell is that?"

My eyes flew open, and I looked up in the direction he was pointing. There, just slightly in front and about 20 feet above the car was what at first appeared to be flickering letters turning counter-clockwise, and I started to comment that it must be a helicopter with an advertising sign, but before I could complete the sentence, my mind had seen the flaws in that scenario, and the object had moved about 30 feet ahead of us. The heat waves that caused the shimmering effect

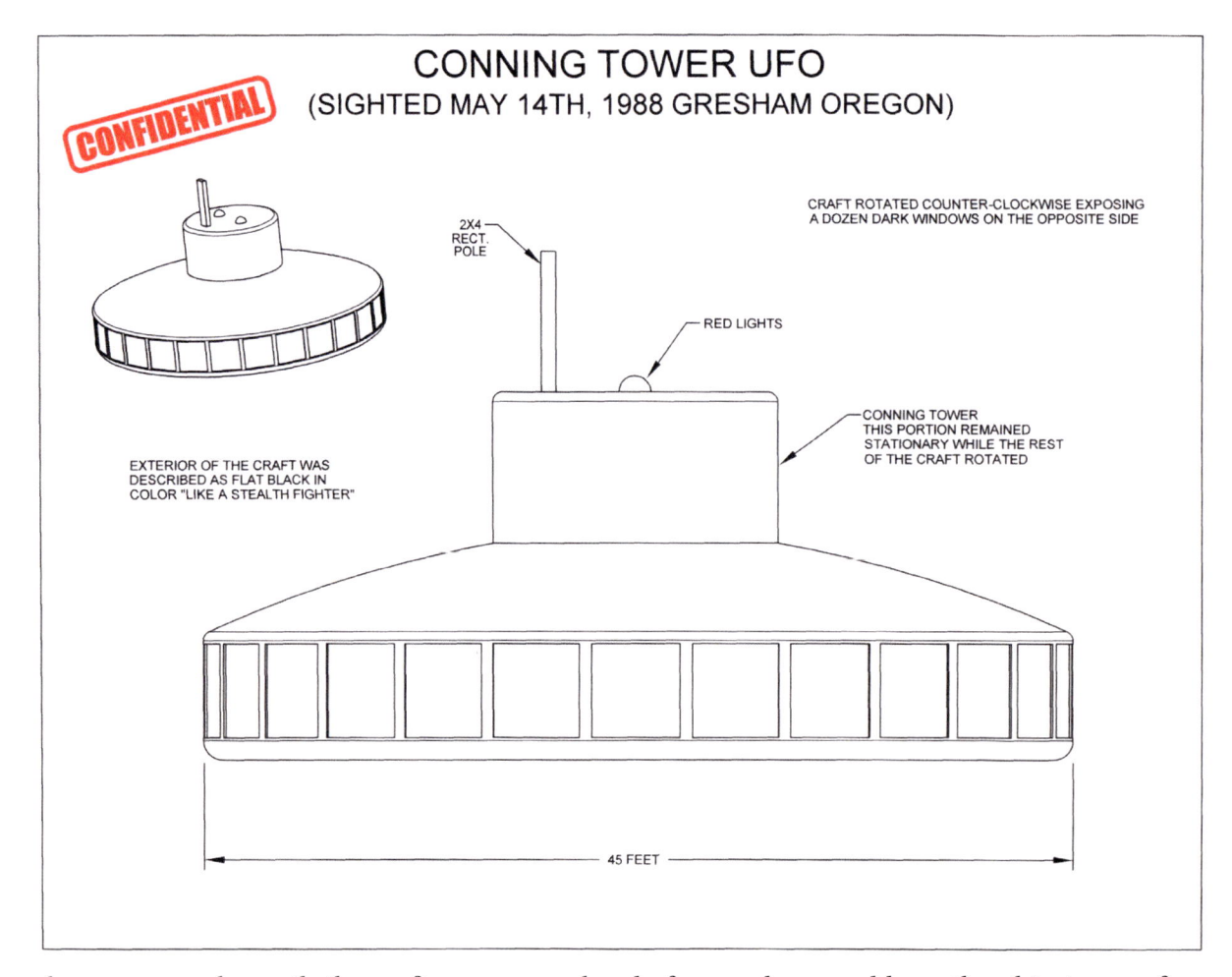

CONNING TOWER UFO
(SIGHTED MAY 14TH, 1988 GRESHAM OREGON)

CONFIDENTIAL

EXTERIOR OF THE CRAFT WAS DESCRIBED AS FLAT BLACK IN COLOR "LIKE A STEALTH FIGHTER"

2X4 RECT. POLE

RED LIGHTS

CRAFT ROTATED COUNTER-CLOCKWISE EXPOSING A DOZEN DARK WINDOWS ON THE OPPOSITE SIDE

CONNING TOWER
THIS PORTION REMAINED STATIONARY WHILE THE REST OF THE CRAFT ROTATED

45 FEET

when we were beneath the craft were now ahead of us, and we could see the object more from the side. What we were looking at was a classic UFO, some 45 feet across (we later figured), with a dozen lighted windows followed by a dozen dark windows as these windows rotated counter-clockwise with the craft about once every 26 seconds. The windows were located on the outer rim of the saucer part.

The saucer seemed to lead us, then stopped across the freeway on the far side of a stand of fir trees. It floated about 10 feet below the top of the trees. When it came into a hovering position, we pulled off the side of the road, turned off the lights, and sat and watched it. We were now on the right-hand side of the freeway— facing east—and the saucer was hovering just across the four-lane highway, and near the top of the trees. This put our view approximately 200 feet from the UFO.

Cars and trucks occasionally passed us, unaware of the phenomenon. "Why aren't they stopping? Why don't they see it?" I cried (to me, this will remain one of the most mysterious parts of the sighting). We could not take our eyes off it. I suggested we make verbal notes of every detail to transcribe later, and we were soon making statements such as, "I count 12 windows before the dark ones appear. It's hard to count as it turns, but – there – see, there are 12 at one time!" Or,

"The part that doesn't turn – that conning tower, is as tall as it is wide." The details that I will relate came from these verbal notations and notes I made as we drove to my home afterward, which was about five minutes from our parking place on the freeway.

When we had first seen the craft and it was directly overhead, there was a faint noise similar to a helicopter. Now looking at it, we could hear nothing. The craft floated in exactly one spot with no up/down or side to side variance. It was round in girth, flat on the bottom, with large rectangular windows about 4-feet by 5-feet on the outside rim. There was space— guessing four to 6 inches— between each window. The light in the windows was a brilliant white, yet emitted no beam outside the craft. The light was so bright we could see nothing inside. The object itself was a dull non-reflective black. Had it not been for the fact that the object was back-lit by the lights of Kruger's Truck Stop about ¾ of a mile away, the dull black portion, against a moonless night sky, would have made the object invisible. As it was, it was in clear silhouette.

The object had what I termed a "conning tower." As tall as it was wide—some 15 feet in width and height, this portion did not turn with the outer portion. It was stationary. This was easily ascertainable by the fact that on the left side, a pole at least six inches in diameter projected upward—around three feet. Two red ball lights were on the flat top of the conning tower. We could see one slightly offset to the left behind the one in front. These lights appeared to be about the size of a basketball, and did not blink. The conning tower appeared to be 1/3 of the entire width of the vehicle.

During this time, Tom and I had discussed his getting a camera out of the trunk. I couldn't imagine that a normal camera could take such a picture at night. Certainly, it would have blurred, but now I regret we didn't try. I was also not anxious to have him out in the open. We had been forced to conclude that we were watching a vehicle from outer space. If it was manned, it was manned by beings alien to us. While we did not feel threatened, we had a strong feeling we were not only being observed, but being considered for some reason.

We continued watching for at least 5 to 6 minutes. Suddenly, the craft began to move upward and toward the southeast. It was headed directly for a large passenger plane beginning its landing approach over Gresham—for its decent into Portland Municipal Airport. Within three seconds, the UFO had risen the approximately 3,000 feet to the plane, circled around the far side behind the tail, and come to rest just under the left wing where it floated in exact position as if held by an invisible thread. We were able then to compare its size: It was 2/3 of the length of the wing. During the time it flew under the wing, the airliner seemed to be fully lit and shiny silver – which I will mention later. About two minutes later, the UFO seemed to tire of that game, and flew back down in a northeasterly direction—coming out just beyond the Wood Village exit. By then, maneuvering to keep the vehicle in sight, we were just entering the off ramp. As we came to the top, the UFO was speeding along the freeway toward Troutdale, about 20 feet above the

Drawing by Rudy Gardea

freeway lights at a speed that must have been 2 or 3 hundred miles per hour. I say that because in the minute it took us to reach the top of the ramp, it was disappearing in the distance.

At this point, we returned home. I made a few notes on the way and more when we arrived. We discussed the encounter briefly, and Tom left. It was not until the following Thursday that the event seemed to come back full force, and we both realized that we should take some steps toward reporting the event. We began by calling the Troutdale airport. They had no reports of a sighting. Portland Airport— same. We were given a phone number in Washington State to call. It was answered by a bored voice who took down the details and hung up. Two months later, we heard of a UFO club (PUFON) at Mr. Hood Community College and attended a meeting hoping that someone aboard the plane the plane had been a witness. Although there was one report of UFOs hovering over a house near that date – it was of a type where the windows were on the conning tower portion. Not our type at all. We came to a blank wall. We could find no bona fide agency to report to.

Both Tom and I had been skeptics of UFOs, and those who reported such incidents, and our emotions were mixed. During those first few days we had to adjust to facts we had hither-to found unbelievable. To accept that we are not alone in this world, that we are being visited by aliens and alien craft, is a difficult transition. It took us from Saturday until Thursday. We could not, however, deny what we had so clearly seen. Nor could we believe that for some unexplainable reason we had both experienced eight minutes of total insanity. We have, as Americans, been brainwashed since birth, lied to by our government, convinced that UFOs don't exist, told that 99% of all sightings are weather balloons, and embarrassed publicly. So, it was with some shock and great humility that we felt it necessary to share our experience. Our friends were…polite. Our families were politely amused and astonished that two upstanding grandparents (Tom was 68 and I was 58), could even think of such a thing. Tom was a retired lithographer, and I was a retired ballroom teacher turned secretary who was soon to get a full FBI clearance in order to join the U.S. Department of Justice. Our friends and relatives knew we weren't liars or weirdos, but it was hard to believe something they had not seen themselves.

After that, we watched the skies, and we knew what to look for. Not only did we never see anything close to the UFO, we never saw an airliner on its approach over Gresham— at night— that shone silver. We must assume that the UFO by some means had lit up the side of the plane. One has to believe that the pilot of that plane saw something, but our nation does not provide a viable atmosphere where a pilot can feel secure if he makes such a report. I wondered if the passengers had reported it, but had no way to find out. I guess if I had one wish about that night, it would be that the pilot would step forward and describe what he saw. In the end, we were left with three bothersome questions: Why are we being observed? Do they all come from the same place? The variety of UFOs seems unending. Where are they staying now? Surly they don't commute to home base every night. Doesn't that last question scare you just a little bit? Wouldn't we all feel better if our government would stop sweeping this under the rug, and begin a search for where on earth they are staying?

SURPRISE LAUNCH AT SEA
February 7, 1989, Catalina Island

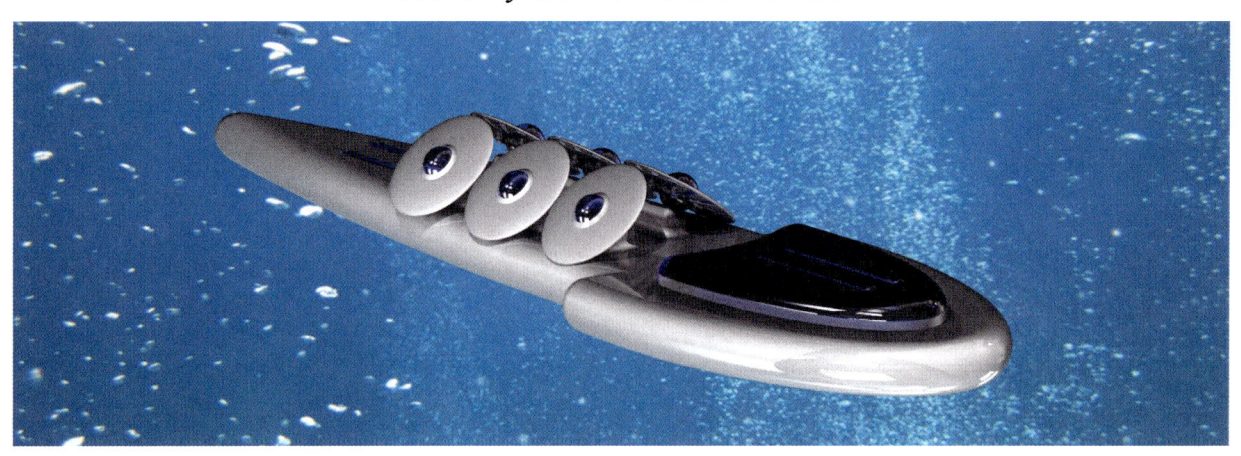

On February 7, 1989 scuba divers, and eyewitnesses on the shore witnessed a strange USO emerge from the water off the coast of Catalina Island. The craft remained on the surface for approximately 90 seconds, and then it released dozens of smaller disc shaped craft from its upper exterior. After about one minute, the unusual craft slowly dove back beneath the surface. [Source: "Undersea UFO Base" by Preston Dennett]

THE FLYING USO ARMADA
June 14, 1992, Catalina Island

On June 14, 1992, multiple eyewitnesses observed hundreds of bright disc shaped lights beneath the water near Catalina Island. The lights were observed for approximately two minutes. Then suddenly, hundreds of saucer shaped craft silently emerged and hovered for a few seconds, then rapidly accelerated into the sky. Reports came in from as far as Malibu and the Long Beach. Coast Guard was notified. [Source: "Undersea UFO Base" by Preston Dennett]

THE FLYING "MIDAS MUFLER SHOP"
November 1994, Buxton, England

Illustration by Michael Schratt and Tom Bogan

In the early morning hours of November 1994 (no specific date given) Mr. "LG" was driving to work along a rural road. As he approached a curve near a bridge that was under repair, he noticed two lights off in the distance. Looking through the driver's side window, he spotted a gigantic machine hovering silently, approximately seventy feet above his vehicle. In a state of shock, Mr. "LG" slowed down and studied the craft in detail. He described it as looking like a sixty-foot diameter disc with a strange "cut out" or notched section near the back. There were two indented headlamps near the forward portion of the craft. The underside of the UFO consisted of mechanical-looking pipes, tubes, mufflers, and silencers. Turning north along a smaller road, the strange UFO paced his car for a few minutes and then vanished in the direction of the Bretby/Repton area. Reports of a similar craft that featured a mass of pipes on the underside also came in from the vicinity of Buxton. [Source: *Burton Daily Mail* February 17, 1995.

Students of UFOlogy will recall that similar mechanical "tubes, pipes and cylinders" were also observed on the underside of the highly documented Hudson Valley boomerang during 1982-1989, the Belgium Triangle 1989-1990, the "Phoenix Lights" case of March 13, 1997, and the Southern Illinois Triangle January 5, 2000. Other eyewitnesses describe the bottom of these craft as looking like a "Midas muffler shop." In many cases, these craft also emit a low frequency "humming" or "buzzing" noise similar to a high voltage electrical transformer, overhead power lines, or sewing machine. What purpose could these strange features serve? Are they part of a liquid nitrogen cooling apparatus for a nuclear reactor, or superconductor?

MOTORCYCLE STALLED BY "FLYING PYRAMID"
1994, Uttoxeter, England

A commuter was on his way to work near Uttoxeter, England, sometime in 1994 (specific date of case not given) when he noticed his motorcycle behaving strangely. Deciding to examine what might be the cause of the problem, he pulled over to the side of the country road that he was travelling on. When he finally stopped his motorcycle, he noticed that he was immediately bathed in a vivid white light. Looking up, he saw a huge square, about thirty feet above him, filled with "superstructure and spotlights" on its bottom surface. Note similarities of "tubes, pipes and cylinders" also identified on the "flying horseshoe" case above. Then, the square dimmed slightly, and began to move away. With a new viewing perspective of the object, he noticed that it was actually a gigantic pyramid, and he had been directly under its base. His motorcycle refused to start, and he was forced to walk home. Subsequent investigations into this case revealed that the motorcycle involved became highly magnetic, and the primary eyewitness suffered from various physical ailments, qualifying this as a CEII case. Source: *Burton Daily Mail* March 3, 1995

EGG SHAPE "PINCER" USO ENCOUNTER.

August 1997, Monterey Bay, CA

Drawing by Rudy Gardea

Moss Landing Power Plant

During a warm August night in 1997, Joy Williams (age 45) joined her husband for dinner at a friend's house which overlooked Monterey Bay, California. The beautiful home was located in the town of Aptos, about a quarter mile from the bay, and was situated high on the hills allowing for a fantastic view. The all ate dinner, and afterward, Williams decided to go outside to get some fresh air. At first, everything seemed normal, but then she noticed a bright yellow/green glow in the water approximately ¼ mile away. For the next few minutes, the glow increased in intensity. Then, a very large "egg shaped" craft emerged from the bay. She immediately called for her husband and their friend to take a look. "It was huge," Williams said. "It was really big…and it was coming out, I could see kelp slipping off it. It rose out slowly."

All three viewed the object in shock. The object emitted no noise. By this time, the strange craft was approximately ½ mile away, and moving north along the shore. At this point, her friend mentioned that she already had a telescope set up, and that they should attempt to use it to get a closer look at the strange USO (Unidentified Submerged Object). Williams looked first, and saw approximately 12 elliptically shaped portholes on the side of the craft. They alternated from green to red in color. After approximately 20 minutes, the object stopped right next to the two tall smokestacks from the Moss Landing Power Plant. The craft was so close, that it illuminated the local area. The smokestacks have a height of 500 feet, and Joy could see that the strange object now was hovering near the circular openings high above the ground. It became clear at this point that the USO measured at least 50 feet across.

What happened next was truly shocking. Unexpectedly, from the right side of the craft emerged what could only be described as something that looked very similar to the articulated arm used on the Space Shuttle. The arm extended out, then upward, and then back down at approximately a 45-degree angle. At the end of the metallic arm was a pair of large "pincers" which began snipping at the rising smoke. The arm extended twice the length of the craft itself. The pincers were about 20 feet long. Both Joy and Tom were shaken be what they had just observed. They would later find out that the Moss Landing power plant had a history of UFO encounters. [Source: "Wonderous, 25 True UFO Encounters" by Preston Dennett]

SAUCER WITH "OCTOPUS TENTACLES" SEEN AT O'HARE

April/May 2001, O'Hare Airport, Chicago, IL

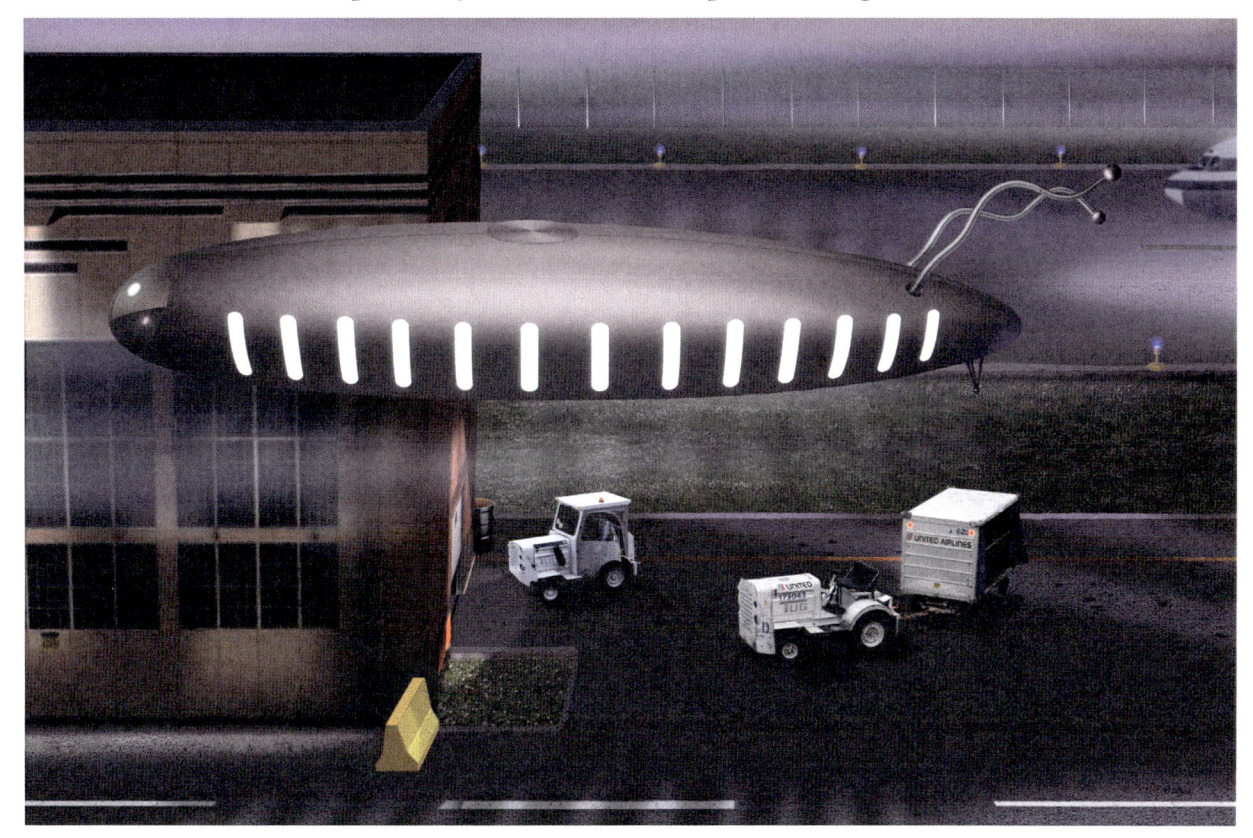

It was 2:00-2:30 a.m. during the time period of April/May (2001; no more specific date was given), when the primary eyewitness (and three additional co-workers) had a fantastic UFO encounter. The source was an employee of United Airlines cabin service at O'Hare International Airport in Chicago. It had recently rained, so the surrounding tarmac near the airport's "Ozark" hangar/warehouse was damp, and a slight fog was still noticeable. All four were facing west near a taxiway, when one of the eyewitnesses yelled out, "What is that?" Approximately 30 feet away, and 40 feet above the ground, they witnessed a circular-shaped UFO pass right in front of them at the rate of 5 mph. From their perspective, it appeared more "cigar"-shaped, but later observations confirmed its saucer-like configuration.

The front of the craft appeared to have two oval-shaped "windows" that were canted inward at a 20-degree angle. It was approximately 50 feet in diameter, and had a silver-metallic exterior appearance. The craft was extremely smooth looking, and featured no rivets, seams or fasteners of any kind. Nearby street lights provided just enough illumination to make out what looked like a "dashboard" in the front "cockpit" (see technical drawing below). There were approximately 12 oval-shaped "windows" running along the sides of the craft which were brightly lit from inside.

CHICAGO O'HARE UFO ENCOUNTER
(APRIL/MAY 2001)

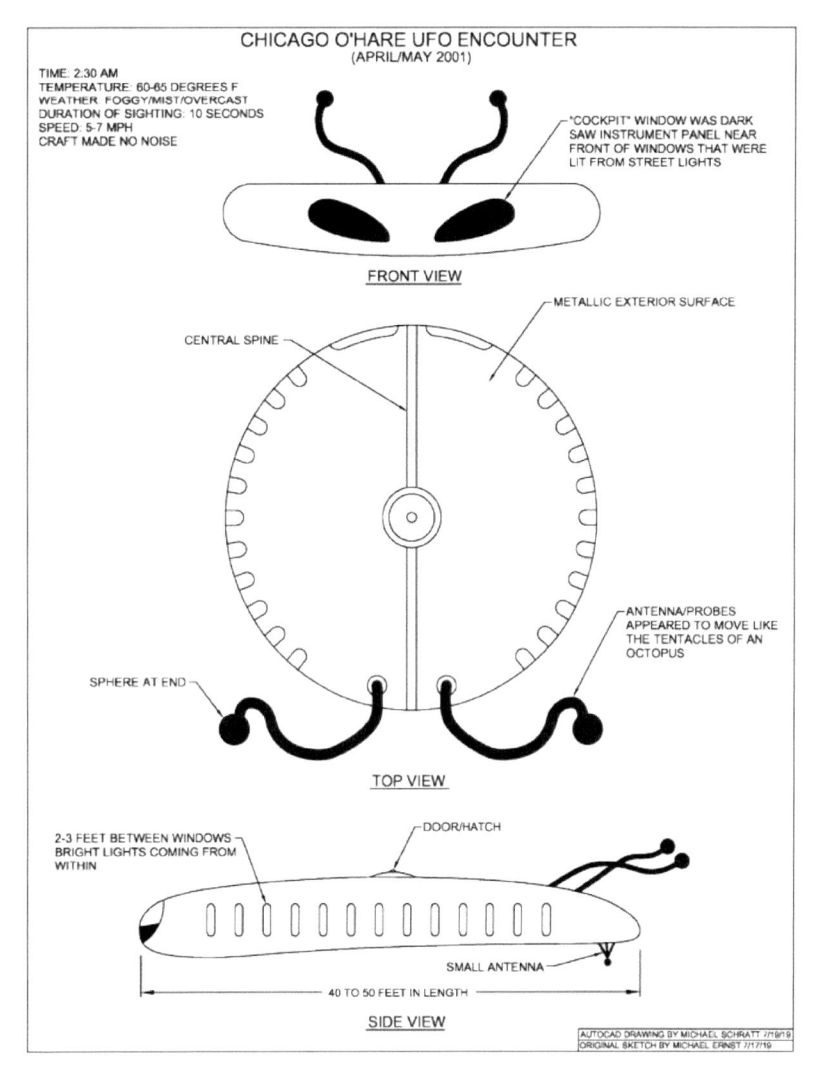

TIME: 2:30 AM
TEMPERATURE: 60-65 DEGREES F
WEATHER: FOGGY/MIST/OVERCAST
DURATION OF SIGHTING: 10 SECONDS
SPEED: 5-7 MPH
CRAFT MADE NO NOISE

"COCKPIT" WINDOW WAS DARK
SAW INSTRUMENT PANEL NEAR FRONT OF WINDOWS THAT WERE LIT FROM STREET LIGHTS

FRONT VIEW

METALLIC EXTERIOR SURFACE
CENTRAL SPINE
ANTENNA/PROBES APPEARED TO MOVE LIKE THE TENTACLES OF AN OCTOPUS
SPHERE AT END

TOP VIEW

2-3 FEET BETWEEN WINDOWS
BRIGHT LIGHTS COMING FROM WITHIN
DOOR/HATCH
SMALL ANTENNA
40 TO 50 FEET IN LENGTH

SIDE VIEW

AUTOCAD DRAWING BY MICHAEL SCHRATT 7/19/19
ORIGINAL SKETCH BY MICHAEL ERNST 7/17/19

Near the aft end of the craft, there appeared to be what looked like two "antennas" or "stingers" sticking out. These resembled "octopus tentacles," and were moving around from side-to-side like they were alive. At the end of each tentacle, there was a 24-inch diameter globe or sphere.

As the craft was passing by, all four eyewitnesses noticed a loud rumbling noise in the background. They quickly turned around and saw a 747 on take-off roll, heading in the direction of the UFO. The strange craft passed the active runway, and tipped up at a 45-degree angle. It was at this point, that all four eyewitnesses could clearly discern its circular shape. They could also see a round-shaped patch or door in the center of the craft, and a long "spine" which extended across its top surface. Eventually, the strange craft disappeared into the fog just as the 747 passed by, avoiding a collision. Source: Personal interview with the primary eyewitness.

THE TRIANGULAR "WATER PUMPER" UFO
2012, Little Pudding River, Oregon

It was 2012 (no exact date provided with report), when the primary eyewitness (Don) saw a triangular- shaped UFO hovering 10-15 feet above the Little Pudding River in Oregon. Apparently, he had seen this craft on four different occasions. The actual location of the sighting appears to have been near Aurora Airport in the vicinity of Hubbard, Oregon. The strange craft was approximately 180 feet across with rounded corners. A few minutes later, a long tube, approximately eight feet in diameter, lowered from the bottom of the craft into the river below. The witness reported that the object began sucking up water from the river into its interior. Then, water would be expelled back into the river downward, and along the outside perimeter of the tube. In addition, three "overflow safety relief valves" also began spraying out water. These "L"-shaped valves may have also served as landing gear legs. This cycle repeated itself multiple times, and the back-and-forth "swishing" noise reminded him of the sound of a "washing machine."

The craft would hover over the water for about 10-12 minutes until the process was complete. Then, it would slowly rise and gently rock from side-to-side as it gained altitude. Finally, when it was high enough, it would zip off at an incredible speed without causing a sonic boom. The upper part of the craft was more dome-shaped, with what appeared to be widows wrapping around the exterior. On top of the main dome, there was a smaller, three-tiered dome, which Don wondered what it was used for. Underneath the craft, was a pale blue light similar to a spotlight that shined down on the area around the craft. While hovering above the river, Don observed a band of brightly colored lights about 10-15 wide that were completely surrounding the middle portion of the craft. These multi-colored lights were moving rapidly from right to left, and then back again. They appeared to be reddish/orange in color.

In addition, Don also recalled seeing three smaller lights emerge from the main body of the craft. These appeared to be orbs, which operated independently from the main object. When the main craft was ready to depart, the three smaller lights would merge with it, and all would disappear together. As he walked towards the craft, he could feel an electro-magnetic field surrounding the machine. Don stated that the hairs on his arms and head began to stand up. During the sighting, his tractor refused to start, and the alternator quit working until the craft was gone. He also reported that his cell phone stopped working. Together, these physical effects qualify this sighting as an important CEII case. During one of his sightings, he drove over to the police commissioner's house, and convinced him to see the craft for himself. The commissioner brought his camera, and began taking many photographs. When the pictures were developed, they appeared completely blank. Don also remembered a story his grandmother told him about seeing something similar nearly 60 years ago in the same place. [Source: David Marler historical UFO collection.]

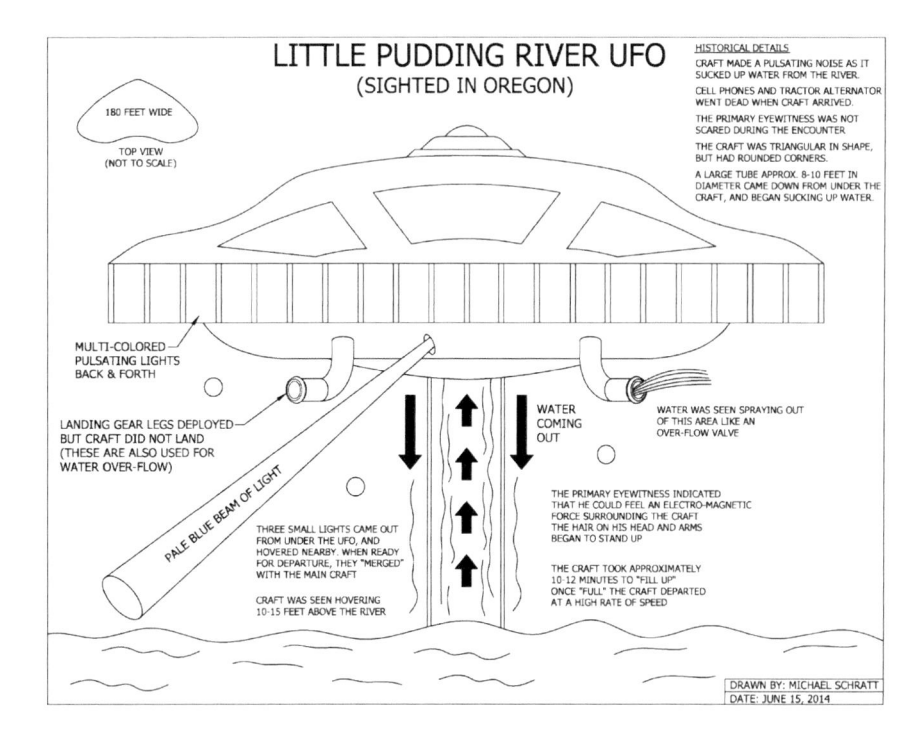

Illustration of the Little Pudding River "water pumper" UFO by Michael Schratt via the original witness sketch.

ABOUT THE AUTHOR

Michael Schratt (private pilot/aviation historian) has been investigating UFO encounters for over 25 years. Between 2008 and 2009, Michael meticulously reviewed a minimum of 50,000 cases which were preserved at the CUFOS (Center for UFO Studies) archives in Chicago. In an effort to maintain an important part of our national history, Michael has re-created dozens of highly credible UFO cases by the use of drawings, illustrations, and commissioned artwork. Many of these include USO (Unidentified Submerged Objects), actual extraterrestrial encounters, and pre-history UFO cases which have never seen the light of day. Michael has appeared on multiple media platforms including the following: Coast to Coast AM, History Channel, Paranormal Matrix, UFO Hunters, Fade to Black. In addition, Michael has been a guest speaker at multiple UFO conferences including the following: Phoenix MUFON, Orange County MUFON, International UFO Congress, MUFON Symposium and UFO CON.

Your questions/feedback are welcome,
Michael Schratt
Email: auroracad5@aol.com

Made in the USA
Monee, IL
12 April 2022